SEMIOTEXT(E) INTERVENTION SERIES

Published by Semiotext(e)
PO BOX 629, South Pasadena, CA 91031
www.semiotexte.com

Special thanks to Hunter Bolin

Design: Hedi El Kholti
Cover image: Lauren Mackler

ISBN: 978-1-63590-243-3

10 9 8 7 6 5 4 3 2 1

Distributed by the MIT Press, Cambridge, Mass., and London, England
Printed in the United States of America

Idris Robinson

The Revolt Eclipses Whatever the World Has to Offer

semiotext(e)
intervention
series □ 38

Contents

To my wife, Mariah, and my son, Langston.

I hope the communists blow you people up, man. You dig?

—Charles Mingus

Writing for the Dead: A Preface

> I write because I feel I am being outraged by
> life. I am *alone* and I am *everybody*, I am God.
> And I write because I take God into my
> wounds and am afflicted by Him and am
> afflicted by all of the absurd suffering and
> senseless bedroom agony of the world.
> —Calvin C. Hernton

Like it was yesterday, I remember standing at Penn Station with my friend from the projects down the street, waiting for the train to take us back to the neighborhood. Not long before this, he had just survived a gunfight, over what was then an issue of dire importance for a hurt Black pride: a basketball game. Trying to pass the time, we amused ourselves with our favorite pastime back in those days: the always entertaining game of laughing at whatever unsuspecting white person might happen to walk by. As clear as day, I can still hear his digression: "Look at them, they kill themselves; committing suicide, who could do something like that?"

With the adolescent need for acceptance inhibiting my honesty, I didn't have the courage to tell him that I thought about it every day—and even worse, it kept me up at night, every night. Now that I'm more comfortable talking about it years later as an adult, the tables have unfortunately been turned on us. As a recent study demonstrates, the suicide rate amongst Black youth has been exponentially on the rise: a trend that has thoroughly eclipsed its white counterpart, which has, inversely, been declining.[1] Alas, it seems that the more bitter instances of history's cunning tend to come with a personal sting.

As for its underlying cause, scholarly interpreters of the data are right in blaming a new sense of hopelessness that is steadily overwhelming the young and the Black.[2] Yet given the current state of the world they've inherited, despair seems to be the only valid response. The dreams and aspirations that had once motivated the civil rights movement, and even certain segments of Black Power, are irrevocably gone and never to return. Think

1. Farzana Akkas and Allison Corr, "Black Adolescent Suicide Rate Reveals Urgent Need to Address Mental Health Care Barriers," Pew, April 22, 2024, https://www.pew.org/en/research-and-analysis/articles/2024/04/22/black-adolescent-suicide-rate-reveals-urgent-need-to-address-mental-health-care-barriers.
2. Janelle R. Goodwill, "Reasons for Suicide in Black Young Adults: A Latent Class Analysis," *Journal of Racial and Ethnic Health Disparities* 11 (2024): 425–40.

about it: Why would Black youth even want to fight for racial equality, only to put themselves on par with a bunch of weird white incel school shooters? Along similar lines, I can still remember supportive members of the Black community trying to convince us that we too could one day become president of the United States; but now that the goal has been attained, these words of encouragement sound all the more ridiculous, mainly because it's a job that no one in their right mind would even want. Indeed, there is a strange irony in the growing acknowledgment that there is just no redeeming this godforsaken country. "For blood pollutes the land, and there is no atonement for land defiled by bloodshed, except by the blood of the one who shed it."[3]

Armed with a copy of Camus's *Myth of Sisyphus* loaded in my North Face backpack, it was around this time that I decided I was to become a philosopher, with the naive aspiration of trying to find a way to think the problems posed by my own material existence. The question as to whether it is nobler to suffer outrageous fortune or take up arms against a sea of troubles came to acquire a rather pressing immediacy in that it followed from the more overt question: What is it to be Black in America? Added to the ever-present fear and

3. Num. 35:33.

frustration, it is to be constantly given unsolicited advice on how to run your life by people of all stripes, cultures, races, and opinions, so that the message is, by its very design, inconsistent with itself. However, there is one common feature that unites all would-be advisors, besides their arrogant insistence on responding to what no one has asked of them: you can be sure that not one of these philistines has read—let alone understood—a single line of Plato. For example, consider this passage from his last and longest dialogue:

> What then is the right way? A person must indeed go through life playfully engaging in a few pastimes—performing religious sacrifices, singing, and dancing—so that it is possible to be able to procure for oneself the favor of the gods in defending against enemies and vanquishing them in battle.[4]

In only a few lines, this divine call to arms exposes the hollowness of all the cheap lies we peddle amongst ourselves just to make it through the day.

Still seeking protection from a hostile world, I went about looking for ideas and concepts as combative as the verses and stanzas forged by the Greco-Chechen poet Jazra Khaleed:

---

4. Plato, *Laws*, 803e (my translation).

On streets and on buses, when people realize you're not one of them, that you're foreign, they look at you with daggers in their eyes. But these people can't touch me. Words are my Praetorian Guard. At a sign from me they leap into the line of fire. Whoever comes at me will feel their spears.[5]

Likewise, Amiri Baraka wanted "'poems that kill.' / Assassin poems, Poems that shoot / guns. Poems that wrestle cops into alleys / and take their weapons ..."[6] Indeed, as Hölderlin once candidly explained, the tradition of the poets has always known that words possessed within themselves a fatal capacity: "The language of tragedy for the Greeks is lethally factive, because the body it seizes hold of does literally kill."[7] Could philosophical concepts deal an equally devastating blow? Perhaps, they might. However, what I got in a university classroom was, instead, the American evasion of philosophy: McCarthyism dressed up in technical jargon.[8]

5. Jazra Khaleed, "A Conversation with Jazra Khaleed," interview by Peter Constantine, *World Literature Today* 84, no. 2 (March/ April 2010): 28.

6. Amiri Baraka, "Black Art," in *S O S: Poems 1961–2013* (Grove, 2014), 149.

7. Friedrich Hölderlin, *Hölderlin's Sophocles: "Oedipus" & "Antigone,"* trans. David Constantine (Bloodaxe Books, 2001).

8. See John McCumber, *Time in the Ditch: American Philosophy and the McCarthy Era* (Northwestern University

It is true, but by no means novel, to insist that theory can only fulfill its own internal demand for weight and determinacy by encompassing revolutionary violence: "Philosophy finds its *material* weapons in the proletariat, so the proletariat finds its *spiritual* weapons in philosophy."[9] Accordingly, this book consists of but a few modest attempts at traversing this distance that separates abstract speculation from the concrete and the real. In fact, most of what follows was written to deliberately intervene in some specific political conjuncture, especially in the context of the hot pandemic summer of 2020.

For example, the first chapter, "On the Black Leadership and Other White Myths," was composed anonymously, as the script for a YouTube propaganda video, written only a week after Minneapolis's Third Precinct police station had been set ablaze.[10] Despite the inspiration for the collective's name having been derived from the

Press, 2001); Christoph Schuringa, "The Birth of Analytic Philosophy Out of the Spirit of McCarthyism," *Jacobin*, January 27, 2023, https://jacobin.com/2023/01/analytic-philosophy-mccarthyism-postwar-communism; and Cornel West, *The American Evasion of Philosophy: A Genealogy of Pragmatism* (University of Wisconsin Press, 1989).

9. Karl Marx, *Critique of Hegel's "Philosophy of Right,"* ed. Joseph O'Malley, trans. Annette Jolin and Joseph O'Malley (Cambridge University Press, 1970), 142.

10. For the original script and video, see We Still Outside Collective, "On the Black Leadership and Other White Myths," *Ill Will*, June 4, 2020, https://illwill.com/on-the-

current hip-hop slang of the moment, the reception of the text was typical of other pieces that I had authored without my signature: in so many words, the overwhelming conclusion was that it was frankly too good to have been written by a Black person. Of course, the criticism was often couched in terms that were far more politically correct, yet no less demeaning. To be specific, there were doubts as to whether someone of African descent would so drastically diverge from a caricature of Black politics, especially in language that was sprinkled with references to psychoanalytic register theory.

After the ceremonial immolation of the precinct, I devoted an entire month to what some might dismiss as riot tourism, but would be better described as militant research into the various ways the uprising was unfolding throughout this immense country. At the beginning of July 2020, I had the poor luck of landing in Seattle, Washington, to find that its previous unrest had subsided into torturously liberal protest marches. Perhaps most indicative of this downward slump was the eviction of the Capitol Hill Autonomous Zone, or CHAZ, which roughly coincided with my arrival in the city. However, the mood on the ground would undergo a dramatic

black-leadership-and-other-white-myths; and "On the Black Leadership and Other White Myths," posted June 18, 2020, by the We Still Outside Collective, YouTube, https://youtu.be/nOFmx8OUnTk.

shift once Donald Trump began dispatching federal law enforcement throughout the country under the pretext of Operations Legend and Diligent Valor. Contrary to the president's intentions, the city of Portland, Oregon, reacted to the repression with a dynamism that ended up galvanizing the rest of the Northwest. Consequently, in mid-July, the specter of the riot had crossed state lines back into Washington.

Around this time, I had the opportunity to share a rough version of "The Destituent Urge Is Also a Destructive Urge" in the college town of Olympia, only a stone's throw away from the boarded-up windows of its recently decorated downtown district. On July 20, the Red May collective organized a similar outdoor public event at the next iteration of the CHAZ, which had been relocated onto the front lawn of Seattle Central College. Since a riot had quite literally swept over the same place the night before, Sean Landis deserves specific mention for clearing away all the debris and wreckage, as well as a handful of used hypodermic needles, in order to set everything up for the recording of "How It Might Should Be Done."

This talk was the first time I would depart from the convention of using a nom de plume for such a theoretico-practical undertaking. Now that I was no longer hiding behind the cloak of anonymity, a few people I knew personally took the time out of their day to tell me that what I had said was stupid. It is an unfortunate fact that those who resist the radical human reconfiguration instigated by revolt remain trapped at the level of spectacular illiteracy, like children lacking basic comprehension, projecting their own distorted imagos onto whatever they perceive. Nevertheless, I was soon convinced that I had made the right decision to use my name, when a slew of less superficial and more unbiased readers reached out to let me know that the topics up for debate in "How It Might Should Be Done" had resonated with them. From then on, I have always reminded aspiring philosophers, writers, as well as comrades, especially those of color, that whenever someone is quick to deride you and what you're saying, then you are more than likely pretty close to being right. On top of that, since it's impossible to win at their game—whether named or nameless—one comes to learn that the best bet is to just refuse their rules entirely and go scorched-earth on the entire playing field.

Initially spoken rather than written, several of the chapters in this book follow in the style of "How It Might Should Be Done," insofar as they are transcripts of conversations I had on the ground. Instead of polished compositions, these were originally nothing more than knotted strings of ideas, extemporaneously deciphered from illegible scribbles in my wide-ruled notebook. A later example of this approach resulted in "At the Encampments": on

April 24, 2024, after a combination of state and local police forces mercilessly attacked a student walkout at the University of Texas, an improvised oral rendition of the text was delivered at the solidarity encampment that had sprouted up on campus in opposition to the repression. However, since the owl of Minerva only spreads its wings *après coup*, these chapters are not meant to be read as mere records of the past, but instead as strategic and tactical proposals for the next rounds of struggle.

It is also worth mentioning that as the flames of the George Floyd uprising faded into mephitic vapors, these texts began to undergo a noticeable transformation, taking on a much more emotional and sometimes even personal tone. This is perhaps best indicated in the chapters "Letter to Michael Reinoehl," "Civilizing the American Wasteland," and "Postscript: On Pain." The change, I think, can be partially explained by two bits of now widely received twentieth-century Black wisdom: "You don't have a home until you leave it," but "Home is where the hatred is."[11] Put in a way that is far more crude yet no less true, you don't know how fucked up a situation is until you start tearing it apart. In other words, the uprising revealed, with a striking

---

11. James Baldwin, *Giovanni's Room* (Delta Trade Paperbacks, 2000), 116; and Gil Scott-Heron, "Home Is Where the Hatred Is," track 2 on *Pieces of a Man*, Flying Dutchman Records, 1971.

clarity, how many of the otherwise mundane and easily accepted aspects of everyday life were, in essence, utterly intolerable. This is, in fact, the rational kernel of Afro-pessimism: it is the characterization of what deceptively presents itself as routine normality strictly in terms of "absolute dereliction"; "for whoever says 'rape' says Black, whoever says 'prison' says Black, and whoever says 'AIDS' says Black—the Negro is a phobogenic object."[12] This is also why, for more than a few of us, the complete and total disorder of rebellion proved to be quite therapeutic and soothing. The same sentiment was poignantly captured by Frederick Douglass when he declared with regard to the sinister complacency festering within post–Civil War reunification: "Peace with the old master class has been war to the Negro."[13]

Another reason driving this major discursive reorientation turns on how the summer of the uprising exposed the permeability of that delicate boundary separating life and death. Recall, at the time, how everywhere, death confronted us all: if COVID didn't kill you for socializing, then you could leave it to the fentanyl to finish you off for isolating.

12. Frank B. Wilderson III, "The Prison Slave as Hegemony's (Silent) Scandal," *Social Justice* 30, no. 2 (2003): 25 (quotation slightly amended).
13. Frederick Douglass, "The United States Cannot Remain Half-Slave and Half-Free," in *The Life and Writings of Frederick Douglass*, ed. Philip S. Foner, vol. 4, *Reconstruction and After* (International, 1955), 355.

However, as the most bourgeois of all bourgeois animals, the American usually does everything it can to avoid the inevitable reality of human impermanence:

> It has been evident for a number of centuries how, in the general consciousness, the thought of death has become less omnipresent and less vivid. In its last stages this process is accelerated. And in the course of the nineteenth century, bourgeois society—by means of medical and social, private and public institutions—realized a secondary effect, which may have been its subconscious main purpose: to enable people to avoid the sight of the dying. Dying was once a public process in the life of the individual, and a most exemplary one; [but in] the course of modern times, dying has been pushed further and further out of the perceptual world of the living.[14]

Yet it was the manifold crises induced by the pandemic that temporarily reversed this tendency by bringing our own mortality back into full and open view. After being forcefully recentered, who can then forget how plague ripped through those

14. Walter Benjamin, "The Storyteller: Observations on the Works of Nikolai Leskov," trans. Harry Zohn, in *Selected Writings*, ed. Howard Eiland and Michael W. Jennings, vol. 3, *1935–1938*, ed. Michael W. Jennings (Belknap Press of Harvard University Press, 2002), 151.

houses of the damned where we warehouse our elders like cattle, or the drone footage of that clandestine potter's field on Hart Island?

At the same moment, the humanitarian logic of the state was exposed for all its disturbing hypocrisy. While the infirm, the vulnerable, the wretched were left to die and then irreverently tossed into unmarked graves, the state's attempt to literally write the neglected out of history was implemented alongside unprecedented levels of control, putatively aimed at "saving lives." It goes without saying that the emergency measures legitimized during COVID were more effective in policing than at safeguarding health and combating illness. With this in mind, we can see through the posturing, so common in the West, that seeks at all costs to maintain the sacredness of life. Yet life is only one side of the dialectic. A life that is unable to risk itself in the heat of revolt, a life that cannot dare death, is not a life at all—it is a living death. Amidst the generalized spectacle of pseudo-life and pseudo-death, the martyrs of the George Floyd rebellion were the first of our peers to cross this threshold.

Therefore, the poet laureate of Exarchia, Katerina Gogou, is right to remind us that even upon acquiring the maturity to acknowledge life's eventual end, the sheer immensity concentrated within a single drop of the martyr's blood can still impart additional weight to the fallen:

[W]e knew
that everyone dies
but some deaths are heavy
because they choose their way of death
themselves.
And we're determined
a death for a death
because we loved life more.[15]

Framing this decision within the context of more contemporary realities, a resistance leader would likewise boldly proclaim: "I say the biggest gift the occupation and the enemy can offer is to assassinate me and to die as a *shahīd* by their hands to the Almighty. I'd rather be martyred by an F-16's missile than die of the coronavirus." Consequently, after the extrajudicial killing of Michael Reinoehl was handed down from the highest echelons of executive power, it became necessary to then seek expressions of thought that might be able to correspond to the gravity of the situation faced by that of the martyr.

It is with the figure of the martyr that everything comes together for us: reason and revolt, philosophical contemplation and practical activity, but in a way that encompasses the entirety of both

15. Katerina Gogou, untitled poem (numbered 13), in *Three Clicks Left*, trans. Jack Hirschman (Night Horn Books, 1983), 28.

life and death, the thrownness of existence and the void of not-being. This book thus repeatedly returns to the question of martyrdom insofar as it opens upon the revolutionary dimension of the classic existential humanist problem. Overturning any division between subject and object, it entails wholly losing oneself in revolt, while at the same time rejecting all the false alternatives that this shattered world presents, whether as capitalist nihilism or religious dogmatism. Indeed, as the words of Muhammad Iqbal show us, it is the path of the *shahīd* that is alone capable of seizing the essence of life in a way that defies its otherwise inherent finitude: "If the self is self-reflexive, self-creating, and self-comprehending, it's even possible that you won't die from death."[16] This is why it is always a mistake to confuse martyrdom with sacrifice, since that which reaches out to eternity can never be constrained by any form of resignation or surrender. More recently, the great thinker of martyrdom Rodrigo Karmy Bolton has gone as far as to characterize its "paradoxical and completely unclassified" auto-affective gesture as "the absolute gift."[17] This aligns with a tradition that has persisted

16. Syed Akbar Hyder, *Reliving Karbala: Martyrdom in South Asian Memory* (Oxford University Press, 2006), 144.
17. Rodrigo Karmy Bolton, "The Absolute Gift: Martyrdom as Destituent Power," *South Atlantic Quarterly* 122, no. 1 (January 2023): 161

throughout West Asia—from its earliest invocations as *Kiddush HaShem* to today's ongoing struggles against imperialism—that regards those elected to spill blood as recipients of a blessing and honor exclusively entrusted to only the most faithful.

So even though I write mostly for the dead, I find that in those rare instances where I do attempt to initiate some semblance of communication with the living, I've tried to reach out to that same Black kid who didn't have the chutzpah to say what he thought on the train platform. To all the kids who "cut their wrists, talking about 'The cuffs did it.'"[18] Today, as is so unmistakably apparent, there are more and more of us. And while the celebration of youth is one of the all too many things about this country that I despise—it is a fascist cult that can only be stomped out by bitter, jaded, and haggard old communists—nevertheless, it's hard not to see the promise in the new generation, if only because they may happen to be responsible for the unlikely fad of Osama bin Laden trending on TikTok.

Nec Spe, Nec Metu
Idris Robinson

---

18. Ghostface Killah, "Malcolm," track 15 on *Supreme Clientele*, Razor Sharp Records, 2000.

1

On the Black Leadership
and Other White Myths

What they call "the Black leadership" does not exist. Let's be serious: what they are talking about is nothing more than a figment of the white-liberal imagination. That is, if these so-called Black leaders even exist at all, then they can only be found shucking and jiving in a "woke" white person's head.

Isn't it interesting how progressive whites seem to have a direct line of communication with Black leaders, while everyone else in the street fails to suffer from the same delusional schizophrenia? What's all the more odd is that the voices that they hear from these magical negroes always manage to say the same things: "Everyone should peacefully protest on the sidewalk, because unmediated Black rage makes others uncomfortable," "Don't strike back at that cop even if he wants to kill you and everyone you love," "I know the manager follows Black kids from aisle to aisle, but still, his store shouldn't be looted." In other words, the message relayed from the sounds on repeat in a white liberal's head is to end the Black revolt and conduct civil disobedience in a manner that is appropriate for Karen and Ethan, not Jamal and Keisha.

It is worthwhile to note that Black people, themselves, never refer to any mythical Black leadership. This is because we know, full and well, that all of our leaders, since Martin and Malcolm, have been killed. Even our potential leaders, like Trayvon and Tamir, are gunned down before they can share with us their vision. What's more, if they are not brutally murdered, then they are locked away forever with Sundiata, Mutulu, and Mumia. That is, we know that if you speak with truth and move against oppression, then the only way to avoid the pig's bullet or penitentiary, the modern-day cracker's whip or plantation, is to go on the run like Assata Olugbala Shakur! In fact, any Black person that says otherwise should be exposed for what he or she is: a poverty pimp!

After half a century without a figurehead in the front, the Black youth has shown the whole country that they are more than capable of setting their own path and directing their own initiatives. They have demonstrated to us a dynamism that can never be reduced to a homogeneous mass following any one authoritative voice. Paradoxically, it is the entire spectrum of the Black revolt in the streets that can be identified as leaderless "leaders," since they have shown everyone else what it means to free yourself.

To paraphrase James Baldwin's still apt observation, we Black people are more aware of the inner workings of our pale-face antagonists than they are of themselves. Consequently, the diagnosis of woke whitey's psychological condition is quite simple: this James Earl Jones, Carl Winslow, or Rafiki from *The Lion King* voice, which bellows off the walls of their skull, is a defense mechanism against their inability to completely repress their own white-superiority complex. What's also abundantly clear is that the only way to fully work through this hang-up is to gain even a small percent of the courage of a Black adolescent and overcome their white guilt with a fist, a stone, and a Molotov cocktail.

2

How It Might Should Be Done

I want to begin with a shout-out to what happened here last night,[1] and to the working class of the city of Seattle, to the rebels of the city of Seattle: I really liked what I saw, that's why I'm here, you know, to feel that vibe. I would also like to send my solidarity to comrades in Greece. It was they who allowed me to experience insurrection for the first time in 2008. The lessons I've learned and the experiences I had there have been so valuable this time around, even though we are in a much different social context. Moreover, a comrade was recently killed at the hands of the police there. To the fallen comrade, Vasilis Maggos, I want to say: Rest in power.

My title demands a little bit of explanation. It is a reference to Chernyshevsky,[2] and to the novel he wrote from inside a czarist prison. Lenin borrowed the title for his 1902 pamphlet, *What Is to Be Done?*,[3] which provides answers to what he calls "the burning questions of our movement": What does it mean to constitute a vanguard party? How do we spread consciousness from this vanguard party to the working class? How do we move beyond strikes to a full-on revolutionary political struggle? Etc. Later, in 2001, a text entitled "How It Is to Be Done" appeared in the journal of the French collective *Tiqqun*.[4] Rather than stating what our goals or objectives should be, *Tiqqun* sought to shift our focus to the means and the techniques of struggle. Instead of thinking about ends, they thought about the means that we should employ.

My aim here is far less ambitious. As for the grammatical construction, "might should," from the southern dialect, I tried to Blackify the title a little bit. But it's also serious, because these are in fact tentative theses and proposals: I'm perfectly OK with being completely wrong about every single thing I put forward today, just so long as it creates a deeper discussion on strategy. What I really want to do is open up this discussion, and I want to leave it for people to engage with it as they want to, and to push it further. At the same time, I want the dialogue to be honest. There's a prevailing posture of cynicism, nihilism, and democratic moralism that holds back insurrection. And I think now *is* the time: we are experiencing an uprising on a scale that many of us have never lived through. Even if we compare present events to Greece, the George Floyd rebellion has gone much further. There are far more martyrs in this struggle than there ever were in the Greek uprising. The time has arrived for strategic thought and reflection.

It's of course weird to find myself saying this in America, the most counterrevolutionary place on the globe. But we must reorient ourselves, and take these questions seriously. The stakes have been raised to the next level—they're extremely high now. It's time for us to think seriously about them. My theses are as follows:

1. A militant nationwide uprising did in fact occur. The progressive wing of the counterinsurgency seeks the denial and disarticulation of this event.

The obvious is not always so obvious.

We all saw it. We all saw what happened after the murder of George Floyd. What occurred was an extremely violent and destructive rebellion. It was a phenomenon the likes of which we have not seen in America in forty or fifty years. Very few of us have experienced anything of this magnitude: a precinct was immediately torched in Minneapolis, after which entire cities went up in flames—New York, Atlanta, Oakland, Seattle. Comparisons were quickly made with the riots after Martin Luther King's assassination. However, I think that we've gone further in this case, that 2020 went harder than 1968, and we're not even done yet.

Despite all of this, the reformists have had the audacity to claim that all of this never actually happened. They are trying to make the burning cop cars disappear, to extinguish from memory the police stations on fire, as if it didn't happen. Again and again, I hear the same script: someone comes on the news, a political activist gives a talk, and we hear them say something like, "The protests were peaceful and nonviolent; they stayed within the bounds of law and order." No: cops being shot at in St. Louis is not within the bounds of law and order. They're doing their best to make the event disappear. One has to wonder what planet they are on that a torched police station appears within the bounds of civility.

This delusion is something that we need to think about. Ultimately, it's more than a delusion. It unites veritably all the progressive liberals who chatter on about what's been happening over the summer [of 2020]. From the Biden Democrats, to virtually all of the mainstream media not affiliated with Fox News, to the Black Lives Matter™ people, the agenda pushed by all these groups is the claim that the insurrection did not take place. I even read a recent study by some sort of consulting firm that sought to prove through quantitative means that there was a very civil nature to the protests.[5]

The fact is, whatever data or graphs they draw up, nothing will erase the fact that police cars were on fire in dozens of American cities. So why do liberals feel the need to jump through such incredible hoops in order to erase this insurrection or this uprising? Why is it that the most violent wings of law and order—e.g., Attorney General William Barr—are today the only audible voices willing to acknowledge that the uprising occurred? We need to think this through.

What is at issue is more than just a momentary lapse of sanity: it is a strategy of denial, a counter-insurgent strategy of reform par excellence.

Unconsciously, liberals do recognize that an insurrection occurred. They can't ignore the shattered glass that occurred in the streets of Seattle yesterday. But what they want is to downplay the significance of these events that mean so much to us, and that we are continually trying to push forward. They want to reassert and reaffirm them, but in a different direction. Ultimately, what they want is to block the possibilities that the revolt has opened up, to dissuade us from going further in this uprising. As with all liberal-democratic reformists, what they're trying to do is exploit the outburst in order to make it so that things change, but only just *a little*—which is to say, not at all.

There's a moral component to this as well, a deep ethical problem. This wing of the counter-insurgency is just one more way that those in line with the system have found to manage and to exploit Black death. It must be recalled (and I will return to this below) that there are scores of young Black children who lost their lives in the uprising, and that activists, "woke" journalists, progressive politicians of all stripes, and even so-called BLM activists are profiting off their death. This is a continuous narrative in American society, and it will not stop now unless we do something about it.

By denying the event, they seek to obscure the revolutionary truth that was ushered in through the streets. They want to extinguish the present that we brought about. They want to sap our energy while they propose superficial palliative adjustments to preserve the system. The history of America is the history of attempts to reform race relations. If they haven't gotten it right by now, they never will.

Whatever they do, whatever slight changes they make, there will always remain an insatiable drive to brutalize and kill Black people. Anyone who profits off this change is complicit in that murder. If you block the revolutionary trajectory of the rebellion, you have blood on your hands. Anyone who remains complicit with the system is the enemy, tout court.

By contrast, the Right has adopted the opposite approach to the event. Besides us revolutionaries, they are the only voices today that acknowledge that the rebellion occurred. There's an illuminating honesty to what William Barr says.[6] Think of it this way: before he can forcefully smash and eventually suppress an insurrection, he must first acknowledge that one did, in fact, occur. In this way, there's an honesty to Trump's words. Trump and his entire Fox News crowd, all those who are calling for law and order, have no choice but to acknowledge the existence of the uprising, precisely because they want to crush it. Just today, Trump declared on the news that he intends to send federal stormtroopers not only to Portland but to New York, Philadelphia, and Chicago.[7] To justify such a choice, he must acknowledge that the uprising did in fact happen. These are the two sides into which our opponents may be divided, the Janus face of the state we confront today.

What is more, the rebellion shows the liberals what it means to defund the police *halfway*, instead of abolishing and outright destroying them. If anyone thinks it suffices to undertake a series of small measures and quick fixes, or that they can reform and preserve the police as a force while simply shrinking it—well, the result is what is happening right now in Portland. Let that be an example to liberals. On the other hand, those who recognize that a change really did occur, and who now seek to stomp it out, are typically more aligned with fascist trajectories and politics, since they are typically the same people who feel the need to dream up and defend a sort of immutable, eternal, and transcendental idea of law, order, and white supremacy. This fascist aspect of order will seek to annihilate anything that deviates from this ideal. For this reason, it is compelled to refuse those same reforms that the liberals attempt to push through. For instance, this is why Trump is so upset about changing the names of military bases. The issue itself doesn't actually matter, but the sort of power he represents cannot stand such changes, and seeks instead to crush and flatten the event itself in its tracks.

There's only one way to deal with this fascist wing of the state: they operate with violence, and we return with violence that's more powerful. However, as concerns the other, more reformist side that aims to deny the event in order to incorporate it into their own objectives, we need to be a little bit sharper in how we handle them. We need to be deceptive, like Machiavelli's fox. Honesty isn't their mode of operating. They have always sought to deny what lies right before our eyes. Deception and subversion is how we are going to have to play them: we need to deceive them twice over.

When it comes to these two sides of the state, I do not wish to claim that either one is any more nefarious than the other, but simply that these are the two sides that we have to contend with, and ultimately to defeat.

2. While spearheaded by a Black avant-garde, this largely multiethnic rebellion managed to spontaneously overcome codified racial divisions. The containment of the revolt aims at reinstating these rigid lines of separation and policing their boundaries.

To begin with, it must be said that former African slaves and their ancestors have been the avant-garde of *everything* in this country. There's no culture in America, in this American wasteland, without us. There's no classical music; there's jazz, and that was invented by us. And besides that, America has nothing to offer the world and it never has.

However, I use the term *avant-garde* in a more specific sense. There were no leaders. We were not leaders of the revolt. We were the avant-garde who spearheaded it: we set it off, we initiated it. What ensued was a wildly multiethnic uprising, and the reformists will do everything in their power to make it so that this truth is erased. If you were out on the streets, you know you saw people of all different kinds. Different bodies, different shapes, different genders manifested themselves in the streets together.

There's a lot of talk about how to end racism, especially within corporate and academic circles. We saw how to end racism in the streets the first weeks after George Floyd was murdered.

It was only after the uprising began to slow down and exhaust itself that the gravediggers and vampires of the revolution began to reinstate racial lines and impose a new order on the uprising. The most subtle version of this comes from the activists themselves. Our worst enemies are always closest to us. You've all been in these marches, these ridiculous marches, where it's "white people to the front, Black people to the center"—this is just another way of reimposing these lines in a more sophisticated way. What we should be aiming for is what we saw in the first days, when these very boundaries began to dissolve.

The most devastating example of how the racial lines and boundaries are reimposed comes from the example of Rayshard Brooks's longtime partner, Natalie White, who offers the most blatant example of this racial policing seen so far. White was called out by so-called "woke" Twitter activists for her involvement in the protests in Atlanta over her dead partner. Eventually, they implicated her in the burning of the Wendy's where Rayshard was killed. It is up to us to never reinforce these sort of bourgeois constructs of guilt or innocence. Whether she had a hand in the destruction or not, I don't judge her either way. That is not up to us; we stand in solidarity no matter what. But I *do* hold accountable, I do place blame on, the wannabe do-gooders, these "woke" Twitter activists who implicated her in what occurred. I lay the blame solely on those activists, and Rayshard Brooks lays the blame on them from the grave.

Order neatly defines collections of people— these are the prerogatives of prison guards, of the police. We should remember the example of John Brown, who was often criticized by his so-called allies and friends for relating to Black people in a way that they deemed unacceptable. If you saw the way John Brown related to Black people in his time, you might think he was being criticized for relating to Black people as human beings. Every time we cross over those racial boundaries and meet each other as human beings, this is when we will be criticized, especially by the most advanced parts of the counterinsurgency. John Brown was heavily criticized for his advocacy of militant tactics, with Frederick Douglass being one of his most outspoken critics. Douglass would come around later, but history would prove Brown right: *the only way to abolish slavery is through violent insurrection.* History has now redeemed him to some extent. But what I want us to think about is this: If John Brown were alive today, what would he be like? How would he behave? John Brown would be in jail alongside Natalie White for crossing over those boundaries.

3. By avoiding the morbid libidinal core of white supremacy, identity politics, intersectionality, and social-privilege discourse comprise the most sophisticated sector of this police apparatus.

We've all come in contact with it at some point, particularly if we have been involved in politics for some time. We all know that identity politics, this talk about "white privilege" and what people call "intersectionality"—all it does is reinforce the racial lines that we're trying to overcome. If it ever had any use or goal, the uprising has superseded it at this point. Let me work through these ideas one by one.

Privilege: I think we all know, or we can all admit, or we *should* admit, that *privilege has become a purely psychological concept.* There's a long history to the notion of white privilege. It dates back to W. E. B. Du Bois, to Theodore W. Allen, to Noel Ignatiev, to Harry Haywood. For each of these authors, what was in question was a theoretical construct whose aim was to incite white workers to strike alongside Black workers. Somehow in the twists and turns that are American politics, the notion became psychological, a way to make white people feel good about their guilt. If you look at, for instance, Peggy McIntosh's definitive text on white privilege, she talks about the privilege of being able to chew with your mouth closed. I don't give a fuck about chewing with my mouth closed.[8]

As for intersectionality: I did a talk at Red May so I won't go into this too deeply here, but as John Clegg and I tried to show, the presuppositions that intersectionality holds are becoming empirically false.[9] What the data is beginning to show is that, for instance, there are more Black women prison guards than there are those going into prison. This doesn't discredit the struggle and plight of Black women, but as a construct, intersectionality is showing its limits. In fact, there are more white women being incarcerated today than Black women, oddly enough. As for Black men, we all know they just sit in jail and stay in jail.

Whatever intersectionality once wanted to do is no longer feasible or viable as a guide for us. In my talk at Red May, I suggested that we get back to the roots of Black feminism. We need categories that understand the Black-feminist struggle beyond the oppression that the system inflicts upon them. I cited Toni Cade Bambara's book called *The Black Woman* (1970): in her excellent preface, she refuses to define what a "Black woman" is. She does not say that a Black woman is the intersection of two oppressions; she does not say that Black women are in the margins of two different systems of hierarchy. What she argues, rather, is that Black women are an open possibility to be further understood through their revolutionary activity. In place of intersectionality as a discourse of systemic oppression, what we need to do is to bring back the idea of Black feminism as *a discourse of struggle*.

Finally, by opening up this definition of what Black women are and who they are, what Toni Cade Bambara was saying was that Black women cannot be tied down by any static identity imposed upon them. Of course they are something *more*. And if we look at the history of Black folks in this country, *we're always something more than what has been foisted upon us*.

Identity politics, intersectionality, and social-privilege discourse: all are modalities of the police.

What's more, and above all, is that each of these discourses ignore the morbid and terrifying libidinal politics that undergirds race in this country. It took someone as courageous as James Baldwin to say this, and everyone is still afraid to repeat it. If you read his phenomenal short story, "Going to Meet the Man," you can acutely see the dynamics of racism in this country.[10] To briefly summarize the story: it starts in the bedroom of a white heterosexual couple. The white man is struggling with impotence. How does he get over his impotence? He remembers back to a time as a child where he was brought to a lynching. At that lynching the corpse was not only mutilated, it was sexually mutilated, and he was given the genitalia. Once he remembers being handed the genitalia, he is able to become erect.

This is deep stuff. No one likes talking about it. But this is the core of racism that we need to reach. What's more, I think no one wants to touch this part of the race problem because we are all implicated in it. It is obvious that white liberals get off on videos of Black murder. It is even more obvious that there are Black liberals who are more than happy to sell these videos of Black death for their own careerist goals. So long as we fail to take into account these libidinal drives within racism, we will not be able to explain how and why Ahmaud Arbery was killed. It had nothing to do with the police. It had to do with what is driving American society as such.

4. **The insurgency cannot be confined within any well-circumscribed sociological category. By necessarily exceeding all classification, it is an excluded remnant detaching itself from all that binds together the American wasteland. Consequently, this combatant formation can only be defined in terms of its movement and its development, as that which emerged during the first weeks of the revolt and which will dissolve itself upon the full completion of the revolutionary project.**

As I said earlier, every conceivable kind of person participated in the revolt. This can be confirmed by anyone who participated in the revolt itself. There is no category that can sum up all of who was there. The best we can say is that what we saw was the inclusively excluded, or the part of America that has no part in it, and that wants nothing to do with this place. Such a formation can only be grasped by how it is moving outside and against the current state of things, it can only be traced by way of its trajectory: against the state and capital, against American society. What is now up to us is to deepen and strengthen this spontaneous organization, so that we come up with something together that is even more terrible, even more powerful than what we saw last night. Something that splits American society in half.

5. The so-called Black leadership, therefore, cannot and does not exist. It is a chimera to be found exclusively in the white-liberal imagination.

You hear it everywhere. I've heard it from every city, every friend who texted me. If I called a friend and said, "Hey, what happened in NOLA?" or "What happened in Chicago?" If there were riots, if people got busy, there was no mention of a Black leadership. If things stopped, if things were stultified, all we heard about was a Black leadership.

The thing is I have never in my life actually seen a Black leader. Why? Because they don't exist. If there are Black leaders, they're dead like Martin and Malcolm. If you're worth your salt, you will be killed. If there are Black leaders, they are in jail with Mumia and with Sundiata. If there are Black leaders, they are on the run with Assata.

There is only one category of people who speak of Black leaders, and we know them as white liberals. The Black leadership is nothing other than a figment and hallucination that exists solely in the imagination of the white liberal's mind. The odd thing about it is that somehow white liberals have more contact with Black leaders than I have ever had in my entire life. It is as if a channel extends from the Black leadership directly into their heads.

There have been reasons proposed as to why the classical formation of Black leadership no longer exists. One argument, which can be derived from many of the new sociological studies (there was a big report about this in *The New York Times*[11] as well), asserts that developing a firm hegemonic leadership of the sort we saw in the past typically requires a substantial middle class. But if you look at the data from the past forty years, the Black middle class has been under constant threat. Hopefully it stays like that, honestly. But it is very hard to define what exactly the Black middle class is. If you do say there is this well-defined group, and if you're able to circumscribe this well-defined group, that group typically exists within the white community. Just to speak a little bit more personally from my experience growing up in New York, I am hard pressed to think of ever having met a Black middle-class person, or of ever having heard their rhetoric and their nonsense. Anyway, it's not really a thing anymore.

Why does the white liberal need to hallucinate and invent a Black leadership for him- or herself? Ultimately, it is because whitey loves property. Property enjoys a special prestige in American life, it has a special kind of sanctity. We always get these calls for the Black leadership from white liberals whenever the windows start to crack. There is a very important reason that property has this particular kind of sanctity in America, as many historians are starting to confirm and argue.[12] For most of its history, the most important property in America was human property, shackled and chained. We need to weaponize this argument, and say that whenever property is protected, it is protected for white supremacist ends. If property is truly the pursuit of happiness, in that trifecta of life, liberty, and the pursuit of happiness, the existence of that happiness and property is premised upon the negation of Black life and the negation of Black liberty. So the protection of property is something that we need to attack explicitly.

6. The current crisis derives from a contradiction that proceeds from the two Janus-faced sides of post–Cold War American governance: an inconsistency between the demands of the sovereign imperial state and globalized biopolitical security. As a result, the metropolitan center has begun to experience the sort of chaos and instability that it has classically sown within the colonial periphery.

This dynamic captures the situation that we are living in today, and which we have been experiencing acutely over the past few months.

On the one side, we have state sovereignty, the classical notion of the state. Following Schmitt, but most importantly following Agamben, the paradoxical foundation of the state proves to be important to the way it operates. The state must employ extralegal and extrajuridical measures in order to found itself. Furthermore, for the state to perpetuate its existence, every time the state founds itself, it must exceed the legal parameters it has already put in place. What has occurred classically, and we have a lot of historical examples of this in America, is that whenever there's a crisis, the state imposes some sort of state of exception in order to reestablish the normal state of affairs that it needs to reassert itself.

As we saw, for example, in the American Civil War, in the two Red Scares, and most recently in the war on terror, the executive branch of the government has continually mobilized itself beyond its formal legal parameters and confines.

We see this today especially with Trump. Trump is using and abusing his executive powers, but it is better to say that he is using them in the way that they were set out to be used. What was originally the province of the legislative branch is now being taken over by Trump himself.

The way the United States asserts itself has also been shown through its involvement in foreign wars. We need to keep in mind, and I will come back to this, that—and for some reason this fact has been downplayed in the past twenty or thirty years—America is the sole imperial power on the globe, and it serves itself aggressively around the world. After the collapse of the Soviet Union and the Cold War, we have seen the US become the police officer, or the storm trooper, of the entire earth. This is one side of governance.

It is important to contrast this with another form of governance, which is typically called biopolitical discipline or biopolitical security. The latter differs from the enforcement of the law carried out by the classic state. Rather, it names the management of lives. If the state kills, biopolitics is concerned with the protection of life—for its own ends, of course.

The most recent regime of biopolitical control is what is known as "security." What "security" does is it allows an event to happen, so as to then manage that event. These events are varied. They can be something like pandemics, like the COVID-19 pandemic we're going through today; they can be famines or disasters like Hurricane Katrina; and they could also be insurrections, like the one we are hopefully fomenting right now. What the state does in these instances is make a statistical calculation and try to find acceptable terms within which it can allow events such as pandemics to occur, while keeping them within neatly circumscribed boundaries.

In addition to the paradox of the state that we see in the state of exception, there is also a strange biopolitical paradox of preparedness that we are experiencing right now. The paradox typically goes like this: after a disaster—say, a pandemic or a famine—there is a drive within the security apparatus to begin preparing for the next disaster to come. After SARS in the 2000s, there was a big push to be prepared for the next coming pandemic. This overpreparedness is then put on the back burner when it comes to light that the next disease is not going to appear when we expect it to appear. The famed medical anthropologist Andrew Lakoff drew attention to this paradox, which we have seen again recently. There has been preparedness for pandemics, but the preparedness was then put on the back burner, so that when the COVID-19 pandemic came we were still not ready for it. We are dealing with two different types of paradox at once here: one where the state must venture outside of itself in order to found itself, and another that involves a cycle of preparedness that consistently generates unpreparedness.

There is the legal side and the statistical side of the state, the nation-state in its classic form and this more global operation of security. I would like to argue that these two directives are colliding with each other and forming some sort of crisis.

Legal means to an end have been in a constant state of crisis: *Trump just can't do anything right.* Whatever he does seems to backfire, and it does not seem to always be the worst thing. Trump and his deluded mind has become an agent of anarchy.[13] Now, of course, he doesn't *think* he is—it is up to us, when this chaos reigns, to utilize it for our own ends. What I'm saying is that we need to inhabit this chaos that the state is inflicting upon itself.

Unlike liberals and reformists, we are not here to reaffirm and reassert law and order. We are not here to transform America into one big safe space. *We are here to make the chaos and the disorder more terrible than it has ever been.*

We must do what revolutionaries have always done: we must make the contradiction intolerable.

7. As the rebel slaves understood with the periodic outbreaks of yellow fever in Haiti, there is a hidden partisan knowledge to be uncovered surrounding the novel coronavirus pandemic that can be exploited and weaponized against established power.

In the Invisible Committee's best book, entitled *To Our Friends*,[14] the authors mention a pamphlet issued by the CDC in 2011 on the subject of disaster preparedness.[15] American Tiqqunists tend not to mention this part. In order to make disaster preparedness pertinent and hip to the youngsters, the CDC invokes the example of preparing for a zombie apocalypse. Their basic argument is that if people can prepare for a zombie apocalypse, they will be able to prepare for a natural disaster such as a flood, a storm, a pandemic, or even an insurrection.

The Invisible Committee argue in their book that this fear of zombies has a long and racialized history, linked in no uncertain terms to the fear of the Black proletariat. And the other side of this fear that doesn't want to be mentioned, that refuses to be mentioned or is repressed, resides in the paranoia of the white middle class over its own worthlessness.

If we look back over the history of zombies, the figure of the zombie appeared within the voodoo utilized during the Haitian Revolution. There was a person by the name of Jean Zombi, who provided us with the word, because he participated in the massacre of slave owners. What I think is particularly instructive for our purposes today is that the Haitian insurgents were perfectly aware that they could use the yellow fever pandemic against their former masters and against the army, whether this be Napoleon's army or the party of order more generally. The insurgents waited until the yellow fever outbreak took hold. They knew that their former slave masters' army would be devoured by the pandemic, and they also knew that they had built up an immunity to that pandemic. So they waited until the army had been decimated by yellow fever, and *then* they launched their guerilla attacks.

What I am arguing for here is something very similar. We all know that Black people and Brown people were disproportionately affected by the COVID-19 pandemic. This is a medical problem. But it is much more than a mere medical-scientific problem—it is a political problem. We must reject the sort of sanitized liberal politics of safety that is afraid of the pandemic, that is largely a sanitary discourse around masks, social distancing, etc. I know this is a political issue now. But, on the flip side, I'm not defending right-wing conspiracy-theorist ideas that the pandemic does not exist, or that it is just a flu, etc. What I'm proposing here is that we develop a kind of partisan knowledge—

our own knowledge about the pandemic—to exploit the pandemic for our own good, and to use the knowledge of the pandemic as a weapon against our enemies.

8. The insurrection will involve precise coordination from within the constellation of riots: the paradoxical organization of disorder beyond any measure of control. Accordingly, the problem of insurrection has equal parts social and technical dimensions.

What I am advocating is a paradoxical ordering of disorder, an Organized Konfusion (for those who remember the rap group). To do this, we must read up on tactics: we must look into what exactly was smashed, what exactly was looted, and how and why the occupations were effective or ineffective. We need to think *strategically* about the chaos that we inflict in the streets.

What is more, we also need to anticipate new forms of tactics, struggles, and strategies that will emerge, so as to intensify these struggles and tactics. We can anticipate that occupations and rent strikes are going to occur in the near future due to the looming threat of eviction that is occurring in all of our heavily gentrified cities. But I think we need to go beyond these defensive struggles and be more creative, initiating tactics that go on the offensive. In fact, what I am advocating here is employing the whole arsenal of proletarian strategies and tactics—from riots to strikes to blockades.

But we need to be creative in our tactics and strategies. As we have seen in the recent Twitter hacks, these are just as important.[16] It also demands thinking about deploying very different strategies and tactics.

What is the modern equivalent of the telephone exchange in Barcelona that was so savagely fought over during the May Days in 1937? What is the modern equivalent of the St. Petersburg rail line that the insurgent workers fought so hard over in revolutionary Russia? We face a unique problem in that we live in a huge country. We need to figure out innovative ways to break this distance and utilize it for our own ends—i.e., as pure means.

9. Materialize the ever-present specter of a second, more balkanized, civil war by fragmenting the fragments of a crumbling empire.

At least since Trump was elected and took office, the archetype of civil war has been looming over this country. There are historical reasons for this. Since the American Civil War was for some the most traumatic experience this country has ever collectively undergone, and for others the most liberating, it stands as a figure that is continually recalled within the collective imaginary. But I think there are also structural reasons for this. The fundamental operation of the state works by warding off the ubiquitous threat of civil war. The state as such can be thought of as that which blocks and inhibits civil war. What is unique about this country is our singular emancipatory tradition, which is itself bound up with our understanding of civil war.

Here I would otherwise cite Kenneth Rexroth's excellent autobiography, where he explains that the radical abolitionists who took part in the Civil War gave birth to children who became the first generation of the American socialist, anarchist, and communist labor movement.[17] But I think the best example comes from Du Bois's classic book, *Black Reconstruction*.[18] It was the proletarian general strike of the ex-slaves that truly put the final nail in the coffin of slavery. It is precisely this lineage of an emancipatory, liberatory, but nonetheless violent, civil war that needs to be updated for its second coming. Another important precedent is Harry Haywood's "Black Belt" thesis. As a member of the central committee of the Communist Party USA, Haywood argued that revolution in the United States of America would involve an independent Black state in the South. I think this is no longer feasible, but I think what he was grasping at, and was trying to deal with, was the problem of revolution in a country that is simply massive.

The revolution here presents a problem of sheer scale for us. This is, I think, why Haywood argued for the breaking apart of America. We have no historical precedent for a revolution in such a large, industrialized, and modern state, so we have a unique problem to grapple with.

I do not know exactly what this looks like. What is certain is that this country is already beginning to break and fracture, and it is up to us to break and fracture it further, into so many pieces that it can never be put back together again.

Revolution, here more than anywhere else, will involve the messy task of division. Here too we have a unique problem, for we must avoid the rather aggressive, ugly, and dangerous nationalism that occurred in other cases of civil war that we have seen over the past forty years. I am not advocating another series of Yugoslav Wars, nor am I advocating what has occurred in Syria. Nonetheless, we must harness civil war as an emancipatory, liberatory power. The fundamental goal is to break America apart into a constellation of federated communes.

10. The fulfillment of the revolutionary project is ultimately an inescapable ethical obligation that each of us has to the dead and the exploited.

At the risk of sounding naive, I sincerely believe that the riots that we have all witnessed, and hopefully participated in, this summer have opened the window to insurrection and even a full-blown revolution. It is possible that I may be miscalculating the potentialities that have emerged. Still, it is entirely impossible for anyone to have participated in the current uprising without having the fundamental core of their being unalterably changed. As for myself, and I know for many of you, we feel the revolution deeply within our souls, and it changes our very outlook, the approach to how we live our lives. All the pervasive cynicism, all the rational self-interest, all the nihilism, *all that is constitutive of the typical American citizen is slowly being worn away by the insurrection and the uprising.*

What this shows us is that the revolution is truly beyond us, truly beyond each and every one of us here. It surpasses all the boundaries thrown up by American individualism. It forces us to finally look beyond ourselves and recognize that America has wreaked havoc as an imperial power around the globe for a century.

And the fight is not only for the living, but also for the dead. We owe the revolution to the millions of slaves who never knew a second of freedom. What the long list of martyrs who have fallen during this uprising deserve from us is nothing other than the completion of the revolution.

Pasolini wrote an essay about a trip he took to America. What really took him was one of the phrases that no one says anymore but was a big part of the civil rights movement: "We need to throw our entire bodies into the struggle."[19] The dead of the struggle scream out for vengeance, and we must avenge their deaths. As Benjamin famously put it, "not even the dead will be safe from the enemy if he is victorious."[20] Tonight is the night to begin to settle accounts once and for all, to end their victorious reign upon the globe, and to allow the dead to finally rest.

3

Race Traitors, Identity Politics, and Revolutionary Horizons Since the George Floyd Uprising (HIMSBD 2.0)

> The horizons which the social revolution in America opens up are more tremendous than anywhere else in the world. But the path which the revolution will have to take in this country is also more difficult and vicious than anywhere else in the world. First, it is the Warfare State with huge forces that have to be challenged. And second, inside each American, from top to bottom, in various degrees, has been accumulated all the corruption of a class society which has achieved its magnificent technological progress first and always by exploiting the Negro race, and then by exploiting the immigrants of all races. ... The struggle to rid themselves and each other of this accumulated corruption is going to be more painful and violent than any struggles over purely economic grievances have been or are likely to be.[1]

That was James Boggs in 1963. And I pulled it out because I think it's amazing how it captures the task that's in front of us today. He identifies the immensity of the problem of revolutionary change far better than any academic or civil rights leader. He's a factory worker by trade. And this is the same question that I tried to tackle in "How It Might Should Be Done." I was never confident in offering solutions, so what I tried to do was to frame some questions and facilitate discussion.

I'll be referencing a lot of people who have worked on the project. In fact, the Boggs quote is from a text that Jason E. Smith wrote a year after the rebellion, on Boggs and the American Revolution, which is excellent. It still amazes me how, in '63, Boggs anticipates Italian Autonomia of the '70s; and there are still so many people studying post-Operaismo, but he's got it in '63. Boggs seems to suggest that the complication that is posed by a revolution in America is how much is riding on it. It needs to be said that radical transformation in the United States opens up unforeseen possibilities for the rest of the world, which has America's imperialist boot on its neck, so that task is also thrown in front of us and makes it ever more difficult.

1. A militant nationwide uprising did in fact occur. The progressive wing of the counterinsurgency seeks the denial and disarticulation of this event.

If you were out there, especially in the nighttime, then you guys know, *it went down*. That is to say, in the slogan that goes around a lot, a militant nationwide uprising did, in fact, occur. But nevertheless there are talking heads who will go on about the mostly peaceful character of the protest. But it's becoming easier and easier to confirm that in the most remote corners of America, it really kicked off. Of course, some of the protests may have been peaceful, but there were a lot where things got a little ill—for example, in the strangest places.

Sioux Falls, South Dakota: They attacked the mall.

Reno, Nevada: They burned cop cars and burnt down the city capitol from the inside (which is a little sketchy, but yeah). In both cases, the governors declared states of emergency and activated the National Guard.

Davenport, Iowa: They had a shoot-out with the cops. It escalated to that, so it's really kind of just backward to say that they were mostly of a peaceful character.

In Michigan, more happened here than I can even recount. Looking through it, I was like, "Wow!"

So I think it's important for us to consider why so much of what we witnessed firsthand can be denied outright. I believe there were martyrs in Michigan during the uprising, so our honoring them means that we have to recognize what happened.

To some degree, the spectacular misrepresentation of the George Floyd uprising as a kind of peaceful non-event can be explained by what Debord called in *Comments on the Society of the Spectacle* "forgeries without reply." I'm going to quote Debord here: "The simple fact of being without reply has given to the false an entirely new quality. At a stroke, it is truth which has almost ceased to exist or at best has been reduced to the status of a pure hypothesis that can never be demonstrated."[2]

Debord argued in *Comments* that the spectacle had achieved a certain level of sophistication once it was able to make it so that something effectively did not happen simply by declaring that it did not happen. I typically will always agree with Guy Debord, but actually I think the present situation requires a bit more nuance.

So I took the lead from a Greek theoretical group called Flesh Machine and Ego te Provoco. They put out a book in 2010 about the Greek uprising in which they tried to chart the way different political positions produce different discourses about violence and how each of them had a different counterinsurgent effect. Alain Badiou's *Logic of Worlds* had just been published then, so that was the main theoretical background for their project.[3] I tried to do something similar with the first thesis.

On the one hand, Badiou separates what he calls the reactive integration of the event. This is the position that's usually taken up by liberals, progressives, everyone from the center to certain sections of the Left. The aim of that discourse is to downplay the significance of the uprising by passing it off as a kind of a civil, orderly protest. Why is this done? This is done to reaffirm and reassert that an event occurred but not an event that constitutes a radical break, so that the possibilities for change are redirected back into the status quo. As with all liberal-democratic reformists, I always say, they change things just a little so that they don't change at all.

So that's the progressive side: the strategy of reform and denial.

The other side is what Badiou calls the occultation of the event. This is the fascist response to the rebellion from Trump, to the Right, to the far right, to the alt-right, whatever right you want, Fox News, etc. In the occultation of the event, they have to acknowledge that an uprising did occur. These were the ones who said, "OK, yeah, there is an uprising." They had to recognize that the uprising did jump off because they wanted to violently repress it. The fascists, the ones out in the street, wanted to bring it down.

Badiou argues that the drive to crush and fully extinguish an event is always done on the basis of some sort of transcendental idea or standard. This could be an immutable notion of, say, law and order, he argues, but in the American context it could be something like white supremacy or the American settler-colonial project, but cast in their positive light, like the American Dream.

Later in an interview with Gerardo Muñoz, "The Revolt Eclipses Whatever the World Has to Offer," I tried to argue that these kinds of liberal delusions about violence and insurrection resemble the Right's fantasies about QAnon, especially after the January 6 storming of the Capitol—they've gotten to the point where liberals deny that certain things even happen. I want to point out the mass looting that's been going on in the past few weeks in response to the Rittenhouse verdict. I think this is a good example of what the liberals try to deny. The Italian Autonomist tradition calls it collective autoreduction. It's been going on for weeks and it keeps being depoliticized by the state and by the media, and separated from the actual political revolt that it's attached to.

2. While spearheaded by a Black avant-garde, this largely multiethnic rebellion managed to spontaneously overcome codified racial divisions. The containment of the revolt aims at reinstating these rigid lines of separation and policing their boundaries.

In thesis 2, I wanted to emphasize that there's something very unique about *the Black experience in America* that was exemplified in the uprising. It sounds like a PBS special, The Black Experience in America, but there's something unique that was shown there. I'm still working on trying to articulate it. But how I tend to see these things is that on the one side, you have America. I keep calling it this vast and desolate wasteland. In *Endnotes*, I recently put out an article to mark the anniversary of the revolt called "Civilizing the American Wasteland." I tend to think of the citizens of America as Debord thought of the planetary petite bourgeoisie. He would describe them as something like, "deprived of freedom, tolerating every abuse, subject to humiliation, cramped and gloomy, ugly and unhealthy habitations, ill-nourished with tasteless and adulterated food, poorly treated for constantly recurring illnesses, under continual petty surveillance, maintained in modern illiteracy and superstitions that reinforce the power of their masters."[4] This is the inversion of privilege discourse. Especially if you read Peggy McIntosh, in a weird way I'd argue that there's times when it seems to imply that Black people want these advantages that white people have. I always try to switch this around and use what Debord said in *In Girum*. He gives a scathing indictment of what he calls "the spectacular salaried masses," or the

French petite bourgeoisie, which he thinks is really lowly. I apply this to all America and say that this country is completely antithetical to anything resembling the good life or *eudaimonia*. And more so, it's allergic to the fine arts and literature; it's allergic to love; it's against communism. Everything that matters in the world, America stands opposed to.

On the other side, you have Black Americans as the avant-garde in this formulation. What I argue, at least in the talk, is that they were responsible for everything in the country that's valuable—every contribution from the beginning. I get some of this from Cornel West on the philosophical tradition in America.[5] But I think it goes further than that. All these valuable contributions that the country neglects even go as far as the fine arts. Ahmad Jamal, the pianist—he lived in Detroit for some time, is that right?[6] Someone correct me. He would say, "I'm not gonna refer to this as jazz, this is American classical music." I think he's right in the sense that jazz is the only American music that can stand on par with European art / classical music.

In this way, I think the Black role was a spearhead in the rebellion. But we're also on a civilizing mission, as I like to call it sometimes. For this reason, I also found it factually false and ideologically spurious to misrepresent the summer of 2020 as a purely Black uprising. For starters, you saw the different people out there. We all know that the daytime and the nighttime actions were very different from one another.

Second, the rebellion itself was nothing other than the overcoming of these state-imposed divisions. As Agamben astutely judged in his chapter on Tiananmen—and I've written about this elsewhere[7]—it's impossible to ascribe a legible demand or goal to the uprising or the movement. The summer's uprising was not about passing some sort of antiracist legislation that was going to land on some bureaucrat's desk and die a stillborn death.

What occurred was what we saw in the streets. What it was doing—it didn't have a goal or a telos. But we saw the concrete overcoming of boundaries as it played out—the alienation that separates us from each other. Agamben refers to this as whatever singularity, as a human that casts off its predicates. For him, this is the strength of the movement: having no demands, the breaking down of identity. The state on the other hand always works to reinscribe identities back into the domain of capture. This is what I was trying to aim at here— this shedding of identities is what the Black avant-garde was initiating.

So you have this clash between the state and the non-state, or as Agamben says, the state versus humanity. I see the Black avant-garde as having this role of initiating the civilizing process that demonstrates what humanity really is in the most inhumane country in the world.

3. The insurgency cannot be confined within any well-circumscribed sociological category. By necessarily exceeding all classification, it is an excluded remnant detaching itself from all that binds together the American wasteland. Consequently, this combatant formation can only be defined in terms of its movement and its development, as that which emerged during the first weeks of the revolt and which will dissolve itself upon the full completion of the revolutionary project.

This thesis is saying roughly the same thing as the previous one, but further relies on constructs from Agamben and Badiou. What I want to say is that identity politics is overcome in the course of the revolt. There is some part which is nevertheless not a part of the American wasteland that is bringing about this change.[8]

4. By avoiding the morbid libidinal core of white supremacy, identity politics, intersectionality, and social-privilege discourse comprise the most sophisticated sector of this police apparatus.

This thesis splits into two parts. On the one hand is the critique of identity politics, intersectionality, and social-privilege discourse. On the other hand, it deals with what I call "the morbid libidinal economy."

The first part of the project comes from work I've done with John Clegg, a scholar of prison and slavery at the University of Chicago. I won't go through all the statistics that he's been working on and all the empirical data that he's collected—that's his side of the project—but I want to give a basic sketch of some of the arguments that I was trying to put forward against intersectionality.

So, to start with, on a very basic level, intersectionality is obviously true. It's correct on some fundamental level. If we follow Kimberlé Crenshaw's[8] original line of reasoning, then we could say something like, "Yes, there is something very unique about a person who's simultaneously being held between two intersecting oppressions. In a way, that's tautologically correct. Yes, it's unique, but what are we going to derive from this?" And you have certain crude models of intersectionality that will argue, whether implicitly or explicitly, that multiple oppressions entail more oppression—something more than uniqueness. But of course this doesn't really follow.

The other problem that I think occurs in both the crude and the refined models of intersectionality is that they'll argue that this kind of intersectional position, this position at the conjunction between two oppressions, this crossing, is what confers agency onto a subject. I also think this is incorrect. This doesn't follow. Just because a group is situated at the crossing point of two forms of domination, this position doesn't make that person or that group more equipped to fight one form of oppression, the other form, or both forms of oppression.

Typically, intersectionality is contested from some sort of class-first perspective. This is not what I'm doing. I always want to make that clear. In fact, in "How It Might Should Be Done," I argued that Marx makes some of the same mistakes that intersectionality makes. He has several formulations of the proletariat. There's some that are really good, but he makes the same mistakes at other times. There are times when he says that the proletariat is the most oppressed, therefore it's the one revolutionary subject. False. There are times when he says the proletariat is located at the levers of production, therefore it's the revolutionary subject. Also probably false.

So what I was trying to do was more of an immanent critique of intersectionality to show that it can't achieve the aims that it sets out for itself.

As for privilege theory, I should make a slight change to something I said in "How It Might Should Be Done"—namely, when I argued that a psychological component has been added to the theory after the fact. Du Bois does talk about a psychological wage of whiteness. Nevertheless, the psychology of the wage of whiteness has been morphed into what Peggy McIntosh talks about, about chewing with your mouth open. Most importantly, it becomes this way to wallow in psychological guilt.[10]

Rest in peace to Noel Ignatiev. He once said, I remember, before he died, that he wanted to give up the term *race* altogether because it's been abused so much. I'm starting to think that he should have said that about *privilege*, even though that was his idea. I tried to go back into the more revolutionary lineage of privilege and look at Harry Haywood, Theodore W. Allen, and Noel Ignatiev. What's important for me is that their formulation entailed that white workers have to strike alongside Black workers. They have to recognize that their real alliances aren't with the white bourgeoisie but with Black workers, and to strike in solidarity with them, recognizing that they share the same class enemy. This comes out to something very different from the crap you get in diversity trainings, which really promotes inaction.

Lastly, identity politics. This is the hardest one to deal with. I've been messing with this for a decade now. I think it's really hard to deal with because, as this philosopher Cressida Heyes writes in her entry on this, it's such an incredibly loaded phrase, and it has such an extremely wide reference that it's really hard to tie down.[11] So it's difficult to construct a precise objection as to what identity politics wants to do, or is doing, or what it stands for, what it holds. It means so many different things to different people.

I even think about it as something that's really deep inside us, a kind of prephilosophical understanding. A good way to think of this can be taken from Cavell's reading of Wittgenstein.[12] He said that Wittgenstein was attacking the urge to do bad philosophy. Likewise, identity politics operates in a manner similar to bad philosophy in that both are prior to theorization. They are both pretheoretic urges that we give in to so that before any systematic thinking even begins, the mistake has already occurred. In other ways, I try to analyze identity politics as a technique of power in the Foucauldian sense. Instead of being one theory, it's a multiple set of mechanisms and techniques and procedures of power.

The overall critique of identity politics will also apply to intersectionality, privilege theory, etc. Each of them works by subjectivating identities and enforcing certain rigid lines of categorization. And so no matter which way you cut it, it's always going to have some counterinsurgent basis, because you have to start from these rigid lines of identity and only then do these conceptual systems get moving.

On the flip side, the insurgent side, the insurrectionary side, there would be the shedding of those identities, the breaking down of those borders. And this is why, in "How It Might Should Be Done," I refer to it [identity politics] as the most sophisticated sector of the police, or the most sophisticated sector of the police apparatus or police modality. Some of this I'm getting from Deleuze and Guattari as well. They argue in *A Thousand Plateaus* and *Anti-Oedipus* that whenever this kind of order is set in place, control becomes much easier.[13] So every time that identity is trapped and combined and captured within the state apparatus, it's also easier to control.

What I try to propose, instead of just being wholly against intersectionality and privilege theory, is to look at this book edited by Toni Cade Bambara called *The Black Woman* in 1970.[14] She wrote an excellent preface and I suggest everyone read it. She never tried to define Black women. The topic of Black women is very interesting because that's what intersectionality starts out with. But she never looks at intersecting oppressions, she never looks at people on the margins of two hierarchies. She's going to argue that Black women ought to be conceptualized as an open possibility, understood through their struggles, their revolutionary activities, and their agency. So she starts at the exact opposite of what intersectionality is doing and works in a completely different direction. In general, for us as Black people, it would be wrong to say that we should be strictly defined in terms of the accumulation of various oppressions, especially because they are imposed from the outside.

The other objection that I advanced against the three conceptual frameworks was that none of them have the resources to account for what I called the "morbid libidinal economy" of race dynamics. I began speaking about these terrifying libidinal drives and desires because I observed that especially after 2020, there was endless talk about race, endless talk about white supremacy, white privilege, the Black radical tradition, and Black liberation. There was so much talk about race, but it seemed like there was always something notably absent and off limits, a kind of taboo.

Robert Bernasconi, the philosopher of race, repeatedly emphasizes that race and sex are inextricably linked.[15] We're starting to reach something, a certain unsaid that's omitted. When we have something like this unsaid, it starts to resemble the Freudian death drive. Or more rigorously, it functions like the traumatic kernel of the Real we find in Lacan. He delineates a three-register theory, and the register of the Real is what we always circle around but can never touch. If we touch it, it'll break us apart. I tried to give examples of the morbid libidinal economy. I started with David Marriott's example—that's where I got the reading of Baldwin from, or at least his book is what led me to go in that direction.[16]

Do you guys know Baldwin's story "Going to Meet the Man," or do I have to recount it again?[17] Tell me you know it. Some of you know it. Anyway, OK, I was super hyped when I presented "How It Might Should Be Done" in Seattle. Then my friend came up to me and said, "Hey, great talk, but how do I explain this story to my teenage kids whom I brought along?" I was like, "Ehhh."

In brief, you have a white heterosexual couple in Baldwin's short story. The setting consists of the man who's a redneck cop, he's lying in bed with his wife. He's suffering from impotence and he's unable to perform. What's more psychoanalytic than impotence? Spoiler alert: he begins to think about a lynching he attended as a young boy. As we know, lynchings are always exceedingly sexualized rituals of white supremacy. The corpse of the Black man is not just mutilated, but it's sexually mutilated. Upon remembering the sexual mutilation, the cop is then able to achieve an erection.

I compared this Baldwin story to the real-life murder of Ahmaud Arbery. I still think this holds—we could work this through a little more, but it's obvious to me that there's some kind of libidinal desire motivating those rednecks down in

Georgia. They were getting something out of it. Otherwise, those hicks could have just sat there on their porch and not thought twice about Ahmaud Arbery jogging past them. Of course, that's never talked about. You don't hear Don Lemon talking about the morbid libidinal drives of those rednecks down there. It's uncomfortable to talk about for a lot of reasons. And one would have to admit that all heterosexual white males in America have some similar impulses. That's why it makes us uncomfortable. I was debating whether I'd say this, but I moved from New York City to New Mexico, and the weirdest thing was not so much being the only Black person there but how much attention I got from white heterosexual men: they'd always be following me around with their eyes on me. On a general level, our society also associates Black suffering with gratification, and that's another way we can approach this.

Additionally, a lot of the influence, a lot of my understanding of the morbid libidinal economy, comes from Hortense J. Spillers's work. She did the best work on this. Her text, "Mama's Baby, Papa's Maybe" is groundbreaking.[18] For instance, she gives a really fascinating interpretation of Harriet Jacobs's autobiography.[19] In that part of the book, Jacobs recounts how she's incessantly subjected to sexual harassment by the plantation owner. His unwanted attention precipitates the jealousy of the master's wife. In the quiet of the night, the jealous mistress enters Jacobs's slave quarters and speaks to her while she's sleeping in a murderous voice of envy. Jacobs is like, "She's going to kill me." And the voice enters into both the manifest and latent content of her dream. So you have a classic psychoanalytic instance. The mistress also begins to mimic both her husband's sexual advances toward Jacobs as well as his threats. It's a little bit of both.

Spillers concludes—I'm just going to quote her because it's perfect—"In both male and female instances, the subject attempts to *insinuate* his or her will into the vulnerable, supine [slave] body. … We might say that [Jacobs], between the lines of her narrative, demarcates a sexuality that is neuterbound, because it represents an open vulnerability to a gigantic sexualized repertoire that may be alternately expressed as male and/or female. Since the gendered female *exists* for the male, we might say that the ungendered female—in an amazing stroke of pansexual potential—might be invaded/raided by another woman or man."[20] Her conclusion is that this degendering of Black flesh serves as the foundation for the white gender binary, which in her view only exists for whites.

These libidinal dynamics do not always have to play out in life-and-death scenarios. I think that there are always less exaggerated instances of these exchanges. You can think of times you'll see a white girl who's friends with a Black girl, and then the white girl is like, "Oh, I'm so cool, I'm so hip-hop now." It's these subtle ways they manipulate their Black friends in friendships. I think it's really prevalent in woke activist circles, but it's not something that's talked about.

Spillers's reading also shows that gender and race are way more complicated than the three calculi of identity points can really account for. For Spillers, the account of Black gender, and Black-female gender in particular, paradoxically involves a degendering. In privilege theory, intersectionality, or identity politics, where it becomes simply one plus or minus an oppression score—it cannot explain something this paradoxical and complicated. And there's another instance, which Joy James brought up in a talk she and I did with Shemon Salam and Wendy Trevino; she said there's another account of a whipping in *Incidents in the Life of a Slave Girl* where the morbid libidinal economy also comes up.[21] It's the scene where Jacobs gets very frightened and disgusted by the sight of a naked male slave body. So maybe we can talk about that.

Anyway, what psychoanalysis teaches us—and it's very interesting that Spillers says that Jacobs invented psychoanalysis thirty years before Freud did, or that she arrived at some of its key conclusions. But what psychoanalysis teaches is that whatever is strategically left out or omitted stands at the core of the system as a whole. The Real is what structures the system; it holds everything together. This accounts for the kinds of defense mechanisms that guard against it. We have various ways of blocking ourselves from touching the Real, whether symbolically or with our material bodies. The white deputization that we saw in the Ahmaud Arbery case is only going to come to an end by traversing the symptom, by beginning at the real core of the symptom.

5. The so-called Black leadership, therefore, cannot and does not exist. It is a chimera to be found exclusively in the white-liberal imagination.

I added in "whitey loves property" in thesis 5. The idea was to remind myself that one of the arguments I made during that part was that property has a special kind of sanctity or prestige in America. If you've ever rioted in another country, it's much easier because people just don't care about windows as much. So how to account for this sanctity of property? Some historians—John Clegg is one of them—argue that property has a particular kind of prestige in America because of the fact that it was once alive. We had living, walking, breathing property.

What I find interesting and what I've been meaning to develop once I finish my dissertation is that there seems to be this interesting shift now. On the one hand, I was in a minority for hating the police. You couldn't say it. Especially in New York, you couldn't say "Fuck the cops"—someone would slap you. But with Generation Z, they all hate the cops now. Or at least it's a little bit more open. And you don't sound like a crazy man for saying "Fuck the pigs." But what's interesting to me is that we've gone from this critique of the state to the prevalence of looting indicating a fully situationist practical critique of commodity, as well as a practical critique of work with Strikeober, but neither has been fully articulated. There has to be a link there, in some way. There's a small step from recognizing that the cops protect the property to "Let's go after the property itself as well."

6. The current crisis derives from a contradiction that proceeds from the two Janus-faced sides of post–Cold War American governance: an inconsistency between the demands of the sovereign imperial state and globalized biopolitical security. As a result, the metropolitan center has begun to experience the sort of chaos and instability that it has classically sown within the colonial periphery.

The next one is thesis 6. So my hero, Simone Weil, argues that war is never fully external.[22] It always has an internal impact on the people who are waging war. What I was coming to notice, especially leading up to the pandemic, is that all these problems that America shifted onto the colonial periphery were starting to come back. The classic Malcolm X "chickens come home to roost." I wanted to give an account of that somehow, and I'll fully get it structured sometime. How I see it, at least in broad strokes, is that in both Foucault and Agamben, you have biopolitical security, and then you have the sovereign state. The sovereign state is always an individual state, or it tends to be an individual state. Then you have biopolitical security, which is a global network. But America is in a strange position because it has the imperial objectives of an individual sovereign state but is also a part of this global network. So maybe that would explain this internalization of war, internalization of all the things America foisted onto other countries in the Global South.

Some scholars have argued that Agamben has never gone the length needed to reconcile the two, and some people have argued that Ernst Jünger's "total mobilization" is a good way to explain how war comes back home.[23] His line was that what marks modern war is of course the biopolitical clash between populations but also the fact that the population needs to be mobilized. This mobilization occurs as much behind the front as it does on the front line itself. That same mobilization can be used later for putting down a strike, or in a crisis, or in the war on COVID-19, or the war on drugs, or the global war on terror. And of course we've seen now the shift from the war on terror to the war on COVID-19. Andrew Lakoff, the medical anthropologist, has argued that even banal terms like "the essential worker" originated in the Cold War, when this was used to designate the workers needed for society to survive a nuclear blast.[24]

One of the ways I looked at this was that Foucault says that the security state or security framework does not block the event, but lets the event happen and tries to optimize it. And with Lakoff's preparedness paradox, we can then argue that whenever we prepare for an event, and the event doesn't happen, then we stop preparing for the event, and then it does eventually occur.[25] We can see it now with the Omicron variant. One of the things Lakoff argues is that there's a reluctance for countries to report that they've found a new strain of whatever virus, like H1N1, since they're penalized for it. So in the next round, no one is going to do it. That makes it impossible to prepare for the next pandemic.

If the security paradigm must allow the event to happen, Lakoff's paradox shows why we periodically get events that exceed the control, maintenance, and optimization of the state.

7. As the rebel slaves understood with the periodic outbreaks of yellow fever in Haiti, there is a hidden partisan knowledge to be uncovered surrounding the novel coronavirus pandemic that can be exploited and weaponized against established power.

The next thesis, number 7, was the one about Haiti. Instead of taking the extreme left-wing view, which is to all of the sudden become partisans of security and biopolitical control, or on the right, this conspiratorial denialism of the facticity of the virus, there needs to be some other way of understanding it. This is very much an open question. The example that I tried to pull from was the example of the Haitian Revolution. The slaves in Haiti were well aware of yellow fever by the time it came around. They had developed immunity, they had developed ways of treating it for themselves. So when Napoleon's huge army landed on the shores, they knew that they weren't going to be prepared to deal with yellow fever, and that's when they launched their guerrilla attacks. At the end of *Security, Territory, Population*, Foucault's 1997 lectures, he talks about these counterconducts of knowledge of medicine that were lost in the middle ages.[26] In Federici's *Caliban and the Witch*,[27] or Carlo Ginzburg's *The Cheese and the Worms*,[28] the miller knows all this secret knowledge that only the proletariat are privy to. This is what I was aiming for in this thesis. It's the hardest to do because you don't want to fully discount all the scientific knowledge that we've been using to deal with the current pandemic. The one great contribution that I've come across is from a biophysicist named Sonali Gupta and Hunter Bolin, who wrote a text in *e-flux* called "Virality."[29] They take up the problem straight from "How It Might Should Be Done." How should we think about COVID-19 without going to extreme poles of total fear or total denial?

8. The insurrection will involve precise coordination from within the constellation of riots: the paradoxical organization of disorder beyond any measure of control. Accordingly, the problem of insurrection has equal parts social and technical dimensions.

Number 8 is the more Blanquist thesis. If you read *To Our Friends*, this thesis is also really influenced by that text.[30] At one point they say, "We're not going to talk about means of production; that's the old way of thinking about things. The real point is one of either controlling or destroying infrastructure." Likewise, Alfredo Bonanno often emphasizes the very materiality of things and not in terms of Marxist value production.

Blanqui is going through a kind of revival, especially since Peter Hallward's new book of Blanqui texts has now been translated into English.[31] It's not just a bad word, to be called a *Blanquist.* There's a certain technical dimension of revolution or insurrection that I wanted to pull out at that time. To think about the equivalent of the telephone exchange that the CNT fought over in May of '37 in Spain, or in 1905 and 1917 in St. Petersburg, the railway was a big, very contested thing. Not because of value production, but because of what it did for communication, infrastructure, etc. At the time I was even reading a lot of books on how to pull off a coup.[32] The problem is that doing a coup in America just seems kind of insane, because it's such a big place. And there's always the complexities of taking the TV station, taking the phone—you can do it in a small place, but in a big place like America it poses a lot of problems.

So this leads to the next thesis, number 9, on civil war.

9. Materialize the ever-present specter of a second, more balkanized, civil war by fragmenting the fragments of a crumbling empire.

At least in radical-revolutionary circles—or whatever you want to call it, leftist circles—this one was one of the most controversial and contested. People didn't like talking about civil war, and just to be frank, it was mainly white readers who really didn't like talking about civil war. I think there's a reason for this. I'll talk more about Nicole Loraux's analysis of civil war, but she argues that civil war is always this repressed kernel in society. It's this trauma that's repressed in the psychoanalytic sense.

My initial reason for taking up the question of civil war was that it was constantly being put on the table. For partisans of the Left, we tend not to read the normal sources that other people are reading, but it was everywhere in 2020 if you looked around. Throughout the Trump presidency, civil war was almost a mainstream topic. Even now if you open up an editorial in, say, the *Post* or the *Daily News*, you'll find stuff on it. I thought that it was something that needed to be addressed if it was on people's minds.

And I argued also—and this comes back to the question of the size and the complexity of America—that civil war would facilitate breaking down America into sizable chunks to deal with in a revolutionary way. We have to remember that during the Chinese Revolution, during the Russian Revolution, they were largely feudal countries. A civil war in America, with this much technological progress, on top of its size—there's really no historical precedent for this. So I argued that the fracturing of America would facilitate revolution. And that we could put the smaller puzzle pieces back together later.

I tried to read this into Harry Haywood, a leading figure in the early stages of the American communist movement. He wrote *Black Bolshevik*, and he also had the "Black Belt" thesis in which he argued that the South should be an independent soviet state, a Black soviet state in the way that Kyrgyzstan or Georgia was in the Soviet Union, a satellite state.[33] And the North would be a socialist state for white people.

The other thing that led me to talk about civil war was that when I was in the Pacific Northwest, it just felt like a civil war. I'm from New York City, and guns are illegal. But I would go to demos in Seattle and I'd see people carrying guns on both sides, and I'd be like, "Oh, all right." Carrying in demonstrations, hiding in bushes when demonstrations were going on, and then with the federal troops intervening in Portland—every day Portland was doing demos, and people were coming from rural Oregon and invading. There was a lot of gunplay out there. It felt like it had the dimensions of a civil war and that's why I put it in there, I thought I needed to address it.

Now, back to Nicole Loraux, the French classicist. I want to go through her account of the concept of *stāsis* in her book *The Divided City—stāsis* being the Greek word for "civil war."[34] However, *stāsis* carries far more connotations than "civil war" alone. In Greek, it can also mean "factional conflict," "partisanship," or "sedition." What I found interesting initially about Loraux's account of *stāsis* in the ancient world is that there are analogous abolitionist and suffragist currents similar to what occurred in the American civil war. Also, again, she takes *stāsis* to have the same status as the psycho-analytic Real. A lot of her analysis speaks about why it is that in the ancient world, once the civil war is over, agreements are forged never to talk about the past. Following Loraux—and also Agamben, who really likes Loraux—these agreements constitute a politicization of the private sphere and a privatiza-tion of the public sphere. So domestic and civil life start to bleed into each other and they become rendered indistinguishable. I think we can see something similar in America today. This is what I argued in the article "The Revolt Eclipses Whatever the World Has to Offer." There's an abolitionist overcoming of whiteness that implies a fracturing of the family, as an *oīkos*. Ever since Trump, a white friend will tell me, "I went home for Thanksgiving and after talking to my racist uncle, I told him I'm going to kill him when the revolution comes." So it's happening! Again and again, this is playing out. In more general terms, Black liberation does entail a forsaking of the lineage of whiteness. And that's what's going on at the dinner table.

Hence the hackneyed saying that civil wars are a clash of "brother versus brother." This is why it became so taboo or controversial for white readers when they read this thesis. They really didn't like the civil war part. Shemon Salam and Arturo Castillon even argue that civil war should be fought within whiteness itself.[35] It should be an explosion of whiteness from within. James Boggs argues that civil war is white versus white, Black versus white, but Black versus Black as well.

On the other side, we have a politicization of the family, a politicization of the *oīkos*. For me, the slave plantation is the paradigmatic instance of *oikonomīa*. This is where the term *economy* comes from. It's a form of productivity within the family structure. It's everything that the private realm was for the ancient Greeks. I think it's obvious that many aspects of American society reflect or exhibit relations that were formerly invested within the system of plantations, especially when the kinds of libidinal relationships I addressed above spill over into public view. The family romances that took on a terrifying turn in the plantation now play out in the public sphere. I work a lot on theorizing destituent power, and what I argue is that destituent power is the breaking of the bonds that keep the *oīkos* and the public so close together. They blend in with each other, and then they're unraveled.

I included the Battle of Antietam in this thesis as well. The Yale historian David W. Blight argues that at Antietam the mass carnage itself was the decisive factor in compelling an otherwise reluctant Abraham Lincoln to pass the Emancipation Proclamation.[36] In fact, it was the single most bloody day in United States military history. However, there was no decisive tactical victory, just a wholesale slaughter on both sides. The mass amount of death was largely due to engaging in obsolescent Napoleonic frontal assaults with modern weaponry. According to Blight, the sheer amount of bodies left behind on the battlefield motivated Lincoln to push through emancipation. Furthermore, Blight makes the interesting claim that no one from Lincoln to the Northern soldiers was, at the time, actually in favor of emancipation. In a way, it was the reciprocal massacre that propelled history to jump ahead of its actors. One of the arguments often put forward against civil war emphasizes that currently the progressive side will surely lose. However, what this example suggests is that winning or losing is not necessarily important for a revolutionary outcome. And this connects to the next part on whiteness and martyrdom.

10. The fulfillment of the revolutionary project is ultimately an inescapable ethical obligation that each of us has to the dead and the exploited.

Thesis 10 deals with political theology. What I've been working with more is trying to understand martyrdom. It continues to be a pressing question. There's the martyrdom of Joseph Rosenbaum and Anthony Huber—they were killed in Kenosha, Wisconsin, by Kyle Rittenhouse, who was later acquitted. Their martyrdom is now in the popular consciousness in some way. I began to address the topic more seriously with my "Letter to Michael Reinoehl." He was hunted down and assassinated by federal agents in the Pacific Northwest. I compared him to John Brown. There's a picture of him during the *Vice* interview, and the look of fear in his eye—it just reminded me of that classic picture of John Brown. So I compared them once it struck me that there's some sort of similarity there.

Stefano Harney wrote to me and sent me some literature on how W. E. B. Du Bois arrived at very similar conclusions about John Brown that I did in the Reinoehl article—I was shocked. And, of course, Du Bois did so much better and more eloquently than I will ever do. In 1909, the same year, he wrote a shorter text called "John Brown and Christmas."[37] It's a little strange, but hear me out. He writes "This is Christmas time and the time of John Brown. On the second of this month [December] he was crucified, on the 8th he was buried and on the 25th, fifty years later let him rise from the dead in every Negro-American home. Jesus Christ came not to bring peace but a sword. So did John Brown."

There are perhaps several problematic aspects of that little poem or passage that Du Bois wrote. But we can do with this poem what Benjamin does in the "Critique of Violence" insofar as he strips the Christian baggage and gets to the Jewish core of the critique of political theology. In other words, Benjamin wants to pull out all the Greek and Roman influences that he detects in Christianity. Agamben does the same thing in a different way, as does Jacob Taubes, when they both argue that Paul really should be understood as a Jewish figure.[38] Relying on Benjamin's notion of pure and divine violence, I tried to explain the act of self-defense that Reinoehl was persecuted for. In Benjamin's "Critique," he insists that even though there's the fundamental commandment that thou should not kill, it doesn't hold in cases of self-defense.

And it's important for people to wrestle with what it means to take someone's life and contravene that commandment. John Brown was such a religious person, of course, he had to wrestle with this internally. What Benjamin goes on to argue is that there's something more valuable to a good and just existence than existence alone. The sanctity of life, this humanitarian sanctity of life, there's always something more than that, and that's justice itself. And in seeking that justice, which is beyond life and death—whether your life or someone else's life—the martyr transforms themself. In this context and in our context, this transformation is what it means to be a traitor to the white race. That's the abolitionist project, and it coincides with martyrdom.

In studying martyrdom, I was going back to some of the early Christian martyrs—Perpetua and Felicity, and Polycarp—to try to pull the theological core out of these narratives. Martyrdom is so misunderstood and brings up so many connotations in people's heads—a lot of the arguments that people threw at me in response to this thesis sounded Islamophobic. In the West, there's a lot of resistance to assuming self-sacrifice. The theoretical side of it that I've been looking into takes up the work of the Palestinian Chilean philosopher Rodrigo Karmy Bolton.[39] People should check him out, he's really dope. He comes out of the 2019 uprising in Chile, and he's a scholar of medieval Islamic thought. He does a lot of stuff on Avicenna. He wrote a great article on martyrdom and he takes up the project that I want to take up, which is how to think of martyrdom in a way that's not fully sacrificial, but that also goes beyond the hedonism of '68. Karmy Bolton explains that the martyr is someone who's totally immersed in revolt.

Anyone who's participated in a revolt knows that in an uprising historical time stops. Linear time gets broken up. Karmy Bolton argues that the martyr becomes unwilling and unable to conceive of the ramifications of their actions outside of that insurrectionary moment. The perception of time is so distorted by the uprising that that person can only conceive of what's going on within the moment itself. Things like their physical, psychological, and financial well-being, all the things that the status quo tells us are important, all become worthless to them, because they can't see outside that revolutionary moment, that insurrectionary moment. This is the theoretical underpinning to that civil rights slogan that Pasolini loved: "You have to throw your body into the struggle." You have to give everything, you immerse yourself in the struggle. To quote Karmy Bolton, he says that "in daring to revolt, the risking of one's life or one's own person in the incalculable intensity of insurrection implies forging a link between the mythic and the political, the eternity of an immobile time and the contingency of history."[40] He gives us a way to understand, to rigorously account for the old saying that martyrdom is a gift. You surrender a life that's plagued by injustice, or a bare life, for something immeasurably greater or more valuable. For good, for humanity. And it's a change of the self.

When I was writing "How It Might Should Be Done," I ended by speaking of these kinds of historical wrongs that need to be righted. The revenge for the dead—the dead of the struggle, but also the dead who never had a moment of freedom. And I want to end here now by saying that when we heed their screams for vengeance, we also fulfill ourselves. It's a twofold thing. It's not just fully sacrificial. To partake in their struggles is to partake in that eternal life that they've created. So finally allowing the dead to rest is the only way we can put our own souls at ease.

4

Letter to Michael Reinoehl

Dear Michael Reinoehl,

I must begin by apologizing for not writing to you sooner. That is, I need to say sorry for not getting this letter to you before it was all over—or better, before they took it upon themselves to end it, and had subsequently finished you off in the process. However, if there is any consolation that we can hold on to in all of this, then it is, as you and I both know very well, that it is never *really* over. And as the old slogan goes, "Nothing stops; everything continues ..."

Believe me, I will totally understand if there is simply no forgiveness left in that big heart of yours, since we all let you down when you needed us most. The sad fact of the matter is that everyone on our side claims to be waiting for the next John Brown, but when he finally appears before us, we instead line up to unanimously reject him. Later on, I think, most will come to acknowledge the tragedy in allowing history to repeat itself, yet very few will have the honesty to admit that you and your children were sacrificed so that we could continue to live our farcical lives of fear and shame.

What I mean is that there will be those who will continue to bear false witness, even though it is impossible to deny that it was none other than ole Brown who manifested himself through you. It is obvious to anyone, who was courageous enough not to turn away, that the piercing stare that the two of you share in common is, in fact, one and the same. Indeed, it showed itself to us, as you sat in that wooded grove, where the unmistakable fire in your eyes made the same silent pledge, which was also proclaimed in the black-and-white image of the great nineteenth-century abolitionist, with his palm raised. It is the look of a person, man or woman, who has declared an eternal war against slavery.

It all happened so fast ... And almost immediately, in the very next instant, so many of those who once stood beside you found a convenient way to forsake those bonds by expressing worries, instead of using their words to strengthen the collective commitments of solidarity. Above all, what indicated the implicit hypocrisy in the whole matter was how quickly they arrived at certain conclusions before they had even had a chance to learn the details of the situation.

The fact that it somehow did not manage to cross their minds that what happened was more than likely a legitimate case of self-defense is rather telling in and of itself. Since the uprising began, the list of those martyred by white supremacists, with or without a badge, continues to grow almost daily: Calvin Horton, Sean Monterrosa, Sarah Grossman, Italia Marie Kelly, Marquis M. Tousant, Malik Tyquan Graves, Victor Cazares Jr., Robert Forbes, Oluwatoyin Salau, Victoria Sims, Erik Salgado ... And in that same week, when you set your course with a bold decision to act, we lost two other momentous figures of your stature in Kenosha: Anthony Huber and Joseph Rosenbaum. Since it is the martyr's blood and not abstract humanitarian life that must be deemed the most precious, I have to accept all of the fault for inevitably leaving out names that demand to be repeated, again and again. Thus, as we witness, with each day, each week, and each month, another human being destroyed by firearms or automobiles, the question then poses itself more forcefully: Why did their initial assumptions stray from the predictable instance of self-defense, which you would later confirm in that final interview?[1]

On the other side of things, there is no Black person—unless they are a complete and total Uncle Tom—who would've even had a second thought about giving you the benefit of the doubt here. This is because the course of our lives has shown us that anyone who plays with guns as recklessly as the fascists do will, eventually and unsurprisingly, get themselves shot. To put it bluntly, if we were talking about an inner-city gang affiliate, instead of a member of the far right, then there would certainly be no discussion about any of this at all.

What the double standard with regard to your situation reveals is how violence in America will always necessarily have a profoundly racial dimension. And it is precisely this—the terrifying core of racialized violence—that they are trying to repress when they lie to both themselves and others that their issue with what you did is a question of strategy or tactics. I mean, give me a break: in a country that is literally saturated in violence, from blind mass shooters to murderous police, no one can honestly claim that the few shots that you let off could in some way be construed as an escalation. There is simply no way to avoid the spiral of violence that began at the very moment when the first wooden ships reached the shores of the Atlantic.

In truth, when considering that a veritable industry has been constructed to promote victimhood—where everyone except the most wretched is capable of cashing in—what they are afraid of is not so much ending up on the smoky side of the barrel of a gun. Instead, what they are really afraid of is having another person's blood on their hands.

Put better, it is what is implied by spilling another's blood that constitutes their deepest fears. It would mean that they would finally have to believe in something—that is, believe in something beyond themselves. Such a choice would necessarily involve a conscious transgression: crossing over a dangerous boundary, at the edge, at the limits, where whiteness ends; and once it has been breached, they could never find their way back.

What I am trying my best to get at, albeit poorly, is what Walter Benjamin had once struggled to explain about the ethical stakes of the commandment, "Thou shalt not kill":

> For this reason, those who base the condemnation of every violent killing of a human being by fellow human beings on the commandment are wrong. The commandment exists not as a standard of judgment but as a guideline of action for the agent or community that has to confront it in solitude and, in terrible cases, take on the responsibility of disregarding it. ... But those thinkers [who raise the objection] refer to a more remote theorem. ... Their argumentation looks like this: 'If I do not kill, then I will never establish the empire of justice. ... This is the reasoning of the intellectual terrorist. ... We profess, however, that higher still than the happiness and justice of an existence—

stands existence itself.' As certainly as this last sentence is false, even ignoble, it uncovers with equal certainty an obligation to seek the basis of the commandment no longer in what the deed does to the murder victim, but in what the deed does to God and to the perpetrator himself. False and lowly is the proposition that existence is higher than just existence, if existence [*Dasein*] is to mean nothing other than mere life.[2]

As holy as they come, John Brown fought, with the utmost religious sincerity, exactly this internal battle within himself. By contravening the prohibition against murder at Pottawatomie, at Harpers Ferry, he drew a line that elevated truth and justice above life itself. It demonstrated that all life will remain senseless and barren, so long as there are those reduced to abject servitude. And yes, Michael, you did the same, when in protecting both yourself and your friend, you brought to reality the chant, otherwise carelessly echoed, that "No Lives Matter Until Black Lives Matter."

Such a conversion of words into deeds inherently involves a fundamental transformation of the self. This is what Benjamin meant when he said that it is more about what is done to the doer than to the victim. Once again, in our context, this has an irrevocably racial significance. To some extent, it boils down to the plain fact that I know so many white people who have never been in a fistfight; but, conversely, when you grow up Black, your grandma won't let you back in the house unless you stand up for yourself and throw hands. It is for this reason that I can so readily dismiss purported strategic concerns as irrelevant, because we are taught to fight even if we are sure to lose to a stronger opponent. In the larger struggle against America, it is clear that, in the same way, we have both nothing to lose and nothing to gain, except for that something "higher" that could only be abandoned by giving in. It's like James Baldwin once said, those who are forced to snatch their humanity out of the fire of cruelty, whether they survive or not, still come to know something that no school or church could ever teach. For others to accept this wager is to perpetrate the ultimate betrayal of their own whiteness. It is to become an abolitionist.

Conducting his raid, John Brown assumed precisely this peculiar blend of hope and despair in order to affirmatively take up his position on death-ground.[3] Accordingly, his willingness to act was wholly reflected in his character. In this regard, there is something about an account offered by the historian Margaret Washington that has always stayed with me:

It's important to understand what an anomaly John Brown was during his time as far as his attitude toward people of African descent was concerned, because John Brown considered himself a complete egalitarian. It was very important for him to practice egalitarianism on all levels. ... And even the [other] abolitionists, as antislavery as they were, the majority of them did not see African Americans as equals. ... Well, John Brown was not like that. For him, practicing egalitarianism was a first step toward ending slavery. And African Americans who came in contact with him knew this immediately. He made it very clear that he saw no difference, and he did not make this clear by saying it, he made it clear by what he did.[4]

For lack of a better formulation, it could be said that *common sense* is very white, whereas *good sense* is totally anti-white.

What this entails is that much of the academic debate about race, which has now become everyday parlance, is actually beside the point. Neither biological nor social, whiteness is to be measured by the degree to which a person clings to the last vestiges of this dying and doomed country. It is to maintain a faith in the same constitutional protections that your summary execution again proved empty. It is to nurse feelings for that one racist family member who still manages to elicit affection and love. It is to believe that a job is actually deserved at a firm where the darker employees can only clean up. In short, it is the extent to which a person embodies life, liberty, and the pursuit of happiness. It is worthwhile to note that, according to this standard of evaluation, it follows that many of the people who are called "Black" must instead be judged as white.

In order to fend off its own dissolution, white supremacist society tells us that there is nothing more insane than the desire to be born with Black skin. This is how they present Rachel Dolezal to us. John Brown was forced to wear this label for more than a century and it will unfortunately be attached to you, Michael, for some time to come. However, this is nothing but a projection of a far more widespread cluster of pathologies pervading white America: a situation in which opiates and self-inflicted wounds have become the only means to temper the pain of rapidly disintegrating personal relationships.

Likewise, the dire emotional state of the individual citizen is being mirrored in the way the country, as a whole, is crumbling before our eyes. To be more precise, I'd say that the American government is doing its best to overthrow itself. Yet, so accustomed to disappointment, I should have expected some of the loudest voices within the movement to express skepticism and a defeatist attitude, and to acquire a defensive posture through their reluctance. It brings to mind the old "Chapter Report on the S.D.S Regional Council" distributed by Up Against the Wall Motherfucker:

A "WHITE RADICAL"
IS THREE PARTS BULLSHIT
AND ONE PART HESITATION.

IT IS NOT REVOLUTIONARY
AND SHOULD NOT BE
STOCKPILED
AT THIS TIME[5]

Despite certain grandiose delusions of white mastery and control, it is becoming increasingly evident that civil war is inescapable. It is not up to anyone. Rather, it is a play of forces that does not need to make any excuses for itself—once the tiger has been let out of the cage, it doesn't go back in without trying to turn its former captors into prey. In other words, it doesn't look like Black people are going to sit down anytime soon, unless Mister Charlie figures out a way to strap us back down into his chair. Therefore, the strategic question is, then, not so much how to stop it, but how to win a civil war.

And so, the misgivings about what you did tend to tread on thin air. What's more, they all turn a blind eye to the concrete lessons taught to us by history. That is, the criticism and apprehensions, which I'm sure you have also heard, tend to ignore the extensive tradition of militant self-defense, which has consistently been the red thread capable of uniting the most advanced and revolutionary sectors of the Black freedom struggle. Only by neglecting this legacy can one mistakenly suppose that racist terror will somehow disappear on its own or be checked by the authorities.

Alas, I have written too much. With that said, if all this is too overwhelming, don't feel compelled to hurry in writing back—even when I don't hear from you, I know that you're still around. To close, I should mention that, in these difficult times, with their disorientating ups and downs, I find myself telling my friends, more often and in earnest, that I love them.

Love and solidarity,

Idris Robinson

5

The Poor Man's Luigi

Though first commemorated in the United States, May Day never seems to do so well in this country. Its rituals are always a lot like how "The Internationale" sounds once it's been translated into English, awkward and liberal. Nevertheless, on a spring day like any other in 2010, I took the J train to the downtown meetup spot for that year's May Day demonstration in that hostile territory somewhere between the Wall Street skyscrapers and the Tombs.

In those days, if there was even the slightest chance for a little property destruction, I would have swum across the East River to watch a hammer find its way out of a Chrome messenger bag. However, the odds for getting into a little trouble that afternoon looked incredibly thin. There were only a couple dozen people in the black bloc: alongside the usual suspects, there were a few suburban kids, clad in tactical gear, looking like their weekend trip to the city was supposed to amount to the final showdown with the state and capital. Also in attendance were, of course, the same reformist unions, political parties, and NGOs: organizations that blended into a wider and indifferent mass of non-violent protesters, which I used to refer to simply as "crowd cover."

Once the march had left with little to no fanfare, I was already daydreaming about what I was going to do after. An old Greek comrade of mine used to say, "When proletarians take the street, if it is not to enact violence, then it must at least make the threat of it." Instead, what was going on that day was the exact opposite: a passive liberal demonstration, the very antithesis of the working class's historical mission. But then, out of nowhere, the crowd cover just so happened to turn left at the exact moment when the black bloc happened to go right. I can only blame this swerve to the left, this twist of fate, this disruption of the planned course of events, on an unpredictable clinamen with no name. In fact, I'd just about given up on the entire prospect of anyone getting busy, when I found myself trooping up Broadway against oncoming traffic, separated from the main march, strictly amongst those masked and draped in black.

I saw the hammers begin to crack! An ATM, a few store windows, and some luxury cars got preferential treatment. *City Room,* a blog run by *The New York Times,* had chronicled the most memorable attack in an unexpectedly sympathetic report: a makeshift hero tried to do a citizen's arrest on someone in the rowdy crowd, only to have his cellphone slapped away from his ear by what the author dubbed "the visible hand of anarchy."[1] All in all, it was a low- to mid-level wild-out, but enough trouble, at least, to have made it worth getting out of bed for the day.

Back in those days, before the George Floyd uprising slightly tamed them, the NYPD had a habit of crashing into a demo while blindly swinging their fists at protesters like it was a hardcore show at Coney Island High. Right before any such attack, there exists a magic tipping point of which every person attending a rowdy demonstration, street fight, or riot must be vigilant. The tipping point is an unspecified window of time when you come to know that everyone has gotten away with just about everything that they can, and all that's left to happen is for the cops to bum-rush the crowd and punish anyone present for having the audacity to enjoy such unmitigated freedom. With practice, an awareness that this moment has arrived can become an acquired sixth sense. However, if you ignore it, you're most certainly gonna get got.

Even though I went downtown by myself, I felt it was only right to inform anyone who might have been marching next to me that I thought it was time to leave. However, convincing someone to quit is extremely difficult when they're really feeling their power. Like "the Great Train Robber," Bruce Reynolds, used to say, it's hard to think about the possibility of getting caught when you're riding high on champagne or adrenaline.[2] The other demonstrators probably thought I was overly cautious, even paranoid; but after saying my piece, I crossed the street, ditched my black clothes, and tried to act like any other civilian strolling through Lower Manhattan.

From a safe distance, I watched the hairy Neanderthal knuckles of plainclothes cops smash into the unsuspecting faces of teenagers and young adults dressed in black. The erratic, unprovoked aggression confirmed all the stories about steroid abuse amongst the NYPD.[3] Dumbstruck, most of the kids, especially the suburban ones, didn't know what had hit them till they were cuffed on the pavement. Against my better instincts, I ran back, grabbed this fresh-faced kid frozen in place, and dragged him into the safety of the nearest subway station.

The final scorecard of May Day 2010 was a few beatings at the hands of cops and even more arrests. The nasty taste it left in my mouth led me to get involved in the solidarity effort for the arrested. The May Day defendants ended up being pretty cool—doesn't Cicero tell us that a life can only be truly lived within the mutual benevolence of friends?[4] And despite all the legal wrangling, things turned out fine. Since they couldn't pin the property destruction on any specific person, nearly everyone walked with summary offenses, roughly the equivalent of a traffic ticket. Everyone except Matt.

The only defendant that I somewhat knew beforehand, Matt ended up, for whatever reason, skipping his court dates. On top of all that, he was the only Brown kid among the group of otherwise white codefendants; yet since he blew trial, he'd be shouldering all the charges. It wasn't anybody's fault, but it just didn't sit right with me.

Thus began an extensive two-year search for Matt across the contiguous United States. When I first met him, he lived around the corner from me, in a tiny Brooklyn studio apartment with about a dozen early twentysomethings piled into one room. I started there, then spread out. Eventually, it became clear that he'd left the city, so I began calling around the country looking for him. Without any real luck, an entire year rolled by. Matt was a traveler kid, so I even asked the street punks who showed up in Tompkins Square once the weather got warm again. The strange, confused looks I got from the crusties were the only tangible results of the whole process.

Over the course of the next two years, a single word reshaped the city's political landscape: *Occupy*. You'd expect me to celebrate this unprecedented event—but this was New York City, not the Oakland Commune. Occupy Wall Street was some of the most annoying petit bourgeois nonsense that I've ever had to endure. A few roommates from the squatted brownstone I lived in went down to Zuccotti Park on the first day, talking about a "second American Revolution." Incredulously, I wrote the whole thing off: "What kind of dumbass Thomas Jefferson shit is that?" At the time, I was working as a bike messenger, but only the bosses were interested in the square occupation, while the other messengers couldn't care less. It was this initial indication of its class character that was the first of many bad signs to come.

Occupy turned out to actually be much worse than I had imagined. The only aspect of the whole charade that I could get behind was the drum circle. Loud, abrasive, and totally uncontrollable, it was composed of all the lumpen and houseless elements that the "serious" activists couldn't figure out how to evict. Their drumming started every day right at sundown, as if they were intentionally trying to piss off both the middle-class protestors and the yuppies living down there in the Financial District.

My antipathy for the Occupiers was sealed when I saw them turn their backs on a march protesting Troy Davis's execution at the hands of the state, claiming they had to remain "politically neutral." Yet I could tell by the looks on their faces that they simply couldn't be bothered about the life or death of a Black man.

To this day, I insist the Zuccotti Park encampment was the first inchoate manifestation of both Trumpism and Bernieism—just as Syntagma Square in Greece led to Golden Dawn and Syriza, and the Indignados in Spain foreshadowed both Vox and Podemos. It was the first protest where I saw American flags everywhere sprouting like weeds, which continues to be a mainstay at both Trump and anti-Trump rallies. The whole ordeal was so irritating that I eventually threw my hands up, filled out a few applications, and went to graduate school. Basically, my decision came down to this: whether it was the movement or academia, either way I'd be surrounded by a bunch of trust fund kids lying about their monthly allowances; but at least with grad school, I'd leave with a diploma to show for all of it.

For better or for worse, Occupy did swell the numbers of that aforementioned tiny black bloc in 2010. The Occupy bug had bitten all the transplant university radicals in the five boroughs who could play revolutionary on mommy and daddy's dime. If you asked them, the upcoming May Day would see the entirety of Manhattan burned to a cinder. A reckoning. I'd be all for it—so long as we leave alone Chinatown, public housing, and a few paintings in the Met—but the night before the demonstration, a close friend came by my crib to ask if I would hold the front banner with him, since the young student-pyromaniacs were too nervous to be at the front of the bloc. Clearly, if you're worried about marching at the front of a demonstration, then there's no chance you'll be the one putting the largest city in the country to the torch. Nevertheless, my affirmative response meant that exactly two years later to the day, on May Day 2012, I was to depart again from a black bloc meetup spot somewhere in downtown Manhattan. The only difference this time was that the preparatory gathering was several times bigger. However, it was unfortunate that the size increase didn't necessarily correlate with any added militancy.

The cops were already waiting by the time I arrived, lined up in the street, hardly concealing the particular excitement they get from the prospect of beating on someone smaller and weaker than them. Barely holding back, the moment we stepped off the curb into the street, the boys attacked. There they went at it again with their windmill punches. But on this May Day, there was an added violence to the assault, perhaps to add pain to punishment because the march left later than scheduled.

Considering that we never really even stood a chance, I figured I might as well amuse myself with the whole ordeal. Since I had already caught a barrage of spinning punches to my face and sternum, I decided to practice some roundhouse kicks of my own. Doing my best Power Ranger impression, I started trying to throw all kinds of jumping spin kicks over the banner. However, in the midst of the most ungraceful Wushu performance ever hobbled together, it dawned on me why I hadn't tried a flying kick since my childhood obsession with Leonardo from the Ninja Turtles: as fun as it is, it's pretty hard to execute; and added to that, you end up looking like a complete fool attempting to do so. Looking like Crouching Tiger, Hidden Asshole, I am absolutely certain that I never hurt anyone, except for myself, with my improvised choreography.

With a huge smile on my face, I then jumped into the air just to land, like a little baby, in the arms of the most Boar's Head–looking cop out of the whole squad of hogs. Of course, he didn't rub my brow and kiss my cheek. But on a positive note, he also didn't piledrive me into the hard concrete. Instead, Officer McDeli Meat launched me like I was a human football, and when I finally landed back on the ground, I was well outside of the demonstration. It really did look like Uncle Phil tossing Jazz out the front door on *The Fresh Prince of Bel-Air*. In fact, this cop threw me with such force and precision that I crashed at the feet of one of his partners, waiting with handcuffs.

Shackled the fuck up in the back of a prison van, I was put next to my homie from Staten Island—who, yes, even though he's white, is still related, by marriage, to a member of the Wu-Tang Clan. He told me that he'd swallowed all his drugs before they could search him. On the one hand, I was worried his heart might burst open right there beside me on the bench seat; on the other hand, I'm not gonna front that I was a little upset he didn't wait to share.

Since it was the Occupy era, a real cast of characters made their way through the system with me. First off, Donald Rumsfeld's grandson was in there with some penny loafers on. For some dumb reason, I thought it was a good idea to pass the time by doing push-ups; but of all people, young Rumsfeld was feeling it, and started getting swole alongside me. Second, Cornel West also came through the Tombs that day, but they kept him in a different cell. When I later saw him in court, I had to say "what up" to him, and he's honestly a really cool cat. In fact, he took it too far and tried to give me a hug. I appreciated the gesture but still rerouted the embrace into the obligatory hug-dap—on some "Come on, Dr. West, now is the time to look hard, and we all know thugs can't have emotions." Finally, this white Buddhist Squirrel Master–looking guy I used to see around the Lower was brought into the cell. He immediately started practicing Wing Chung right there in the lockup, so I asked him to teach us some stuff. Even better, he convinced everyone to follow him in a guided meditation. For some reason, his Zen powers scared the cops half to death. Maybe they thought he was going to telekinetically toss all their donuts in the trash can. Either way, they hurriedly opened the gates, rushed in with panic written all over their faces, and escorted the great Squirrel Master into the next cell over.

Since there were no windows, I assumed it was sometime around 3 a.m. when everyone finally resigned themselves to sleeping on whatever unsanitary hard surface they could find. Just as the buzz of the different snoring tempos synced up into one annoying hum of white noise, a scream shattered the calm and woke everyone up!

Bouncing off nothing but concrete and steel, the shrieks of human terror and agony were amplified. After childhood play on a schoolyard, it becomes increasingly rare to hear another person scream. What's even more jarring is when the screaming itself is incomprehensible and wordless, because the source of the anguish doesn't make itself immediately apparent.

But the inarticulate scream was a distinctive kind that anyone who has spent a night or two in a holding cell is familiar with. It sounded just like Hubert Selby Jr. had described it in *Requiem for a Dream*: like a man who believes he could die at any moment, but whose noise is then punctuated by whimpers of fear about the possibility of instead surviving through the pain.[5] Without a doubt, what brought us all back to waking reality was the horrendous vocalizations of someone having opiate withdrawals.

Some of the younger kids looked like they might as well have heard a ghost wailing in the night. But truth be told, being totally dope sick while at the mercy of the law is infinitely scarier than anything supernatural.

I was released the next day. The case was soon after dismissed without any legal hassle. What were they going to charge me with anyway, being too big to ask Officer McDeli Meat for a piggyback ride? When I walked out of 100 Centre Street, a few comrades were waiting for me with my favorite post-jail meal: a pack of Newports and a bag of Twizzlers. In between my feverish inhaling and chomping, someone pointed out a street punk picking his nose while walking out of the same glass doors I had just passed through. Considering the placement of his finger, I couldn't help thinking he looked like one of those bad-guy punks from an '80s video game. At the same time, I overheard whispers that this *Streets of Rage* / *Double Dragon* / Rocksteady & Bebop type villain was the same guy going through the sweats the night before.

There's nothing all that astounding about a punk getting wrapped up in heroin, as the two have gone hand in hand since way before Sid Vicious overdosed in Greenwich Village. What amazed me, though, was who walked beside him: Matt. That's right: literally two years and a day after he'd been arrested at a previous May Day demo, there he was strolling out of Manhattan Criminal Court, basking in his newfound freedom.

I couldn't believe it. I ran right up to Matt and fired off a million questions, but most importantly where the hell he'd been for two years. He explained that he had ditched trial to go traveling, hopping trains and hitchhiking until he washed up back in New York in the spring of 2012. With no money for a MetroCard, he had gotten busted for hopping the subway turnstile. When the cops ran his info, the crackers decided to take him in on his open warrants. The poor guy wound up doing over a month on Rikers Island for what would've been a non-criminal violation. By sheer coincidence, he was released at the same time and place that I was—exactly 732 days later.

The entire sequence of events felt too fortuitous for me to leave it at the brief chat we had outside the jail. Plus, as I informed him, I'd been looking for him for almost exactly two years. I wanted some kind of cosmic payoff for my labor. Above all, the best reward would be a chance to hang out with Matt and hear what he'd been up to for so long. He mentioned he was living in a squat and said that I should check it out. We exchanged numbers and planned to get together in the coming days.

But things can never be that simple. A day or two later, I called the number Matt gave me, only to get an automated message saying it had been disconnected. This motherfucker. Well, what are you gonna do?

As months passed, I spent the summer on my bike, delivering food to the hipsters, who were already being boxed out by the yuppies that have since completely infested Williamsburg. Even in late August, the New York heat mixed with the humidity was unforgiving, and riding late into the night left a layer of hot-city muck stuck to my skin.

One night around 10 p.m., leaving a drop-off on a quieter street near the bridge, I heard someone call my name. What do you know—it was

Matt, wandering nowhere in particular with that same insouciant stride that I'd seen carry him out of the court complex a few months earlier.

Matt said he was heading out traveling again, so we agreed to meet up after my shift. I offered to buy him a beer, but he suggested we go check out the squat instead. He gave me another number, swearing this one worked. But I insisted we set a time and place to meet once I finished dragging around food for the young, dumb, and privileged.

It wasn't intentional, but our plan corresponded all too perfectly with a Yasiin Bey lyric: "I'm Blacker than midnight on Broadway and Myrtle."[6] But to me, this intersection always brought to mind a different reference—this lovely passage from Guy Debord's *Panegyric*:

> The greater part of the time I lived in Paris; specifically, within the triangle defined by the intersections of Rue Saint-Jacques and Rue Royer-Collard, Rue Saint-Martin and Rue Greneta, and Rue du Bae and Rue de Commailles. Indeed, I spent my days and nights in this limited space and the narrow border zone that is its immediate extension— most often on its eastern side, more rarely on its northwestern side.
>
> Never, or hardly ever, would I have left this area, which suited me perfectly, if a few

historical necessities had not several times obliged me to do so.[7]

Similar to how Debord once viewed that tiny stretch of the capital of the nineteenth century, I once considered this little section of the twentieth century's capital to be the very center of the universe.[8] You can't really blame me—the Myrtle–Broadway stop was home to the infamous Big Boy Deli, the same one that caused an international incident by selling rotten K2 to Spice aficionados, who then vomited in unison on every corner of the junction.[9] Of course, I no longer deem it the focal point of all existence, because, like Debord once said of Paris, New York City has been "sacked" and "ravaged." The only difference was that the city somehow lost the battle before the fight even started.

Back then, though, it was a good-enough spot as any for a post-midnight rendezvous. Matt was late, so I tried his new number with no more success than the previous one. I ended up milling around the 24-7 bodegas until Matt finally sidled up, claiming his phone had died.

The first squat Matt took me to was only a few blocks away. I use the term "squat" loosely, since it was a gutted, roofless shell of a building that reeked so strongly of piss you could almost see how it seeped into the pores of the concrete. I must have worn my disappointment on my face, because Matt picked up on it immediately.

Somewhat embarrassed, Matt explained that the place was just where he and his friends hung out and drank, but they actually lived in another squat further away. So we set off into the night. I moved along shoulder to shoulder with him, my hand on the seat of my Bianchi, as he began to fill me in on the last two years of his life. Maybe it was the fatigue from my shift or the beer I'd had afterward, but I struggled to follow what he was saying.

As we made our way deeper into Brooklyn, Matt finally told me, flat out, that he'd been hearing voices. It wasn't the first, nor the last, time someone confessed that to me. But even considering all the weird twists and turns with this guy, I didn't see that one coming. What made it even more startling is that he divulged this information to me right as we crossed from Bedford-Stuyvesant into Brownsville: from "Do or Die" to "Never Ran, Never Will." Nervously checking my phone, I saw it was around 3 a.m., which we used to affectionately call "felony hour." That was when I really started to get the feeling that I was in for some shit.

We arrived at a block I'd never been to before and haven't been back to since. We approached a row house that looked perfectly normal. To the right of the front stoop, Matt started prying up a huge stone jammed into the corner where the wall met the ground. Once the stone was removed, he immediately dove feetfirst into the exposed hole. To this day, I wonder why I didn't hesitate, but I jumped right in after him.

It was pitch-black. The kind of darkness that scares any New Yorker raised under the constant vigil of light pollution. All I knew was that since the layout of every Brooklyn row house is the same, I was standing in the basement. But that's all I knew. I couldn't even tell if Matt was next to me.

After standing still for a few seconds that felt like hours, a blue light split the darkness. Then more flickers—blue, orange—broke the dark, and I caught the taste of plastic smoke. Lit up by strobe lights, gaunt and toothless faces emerged, contorted in overwhelming pain and pleasure. Yes, I had stumbled into a group of people sitting in the dark, smoking crack! "And if there's crack in the basement, crackheads stand adjacent …"[10]

"This way," Matt said, grabbing my arm and leading me up the stairs to the ground floor. My very first step at the top of the stairway made the sound of a loud, unforgettable crunch. It was the sound of trampling over the plastic, glass, and metal accoutrements of heroin addiction. I had made my way up from a crack house into a full-on shooting gallery. Needles were everywhere! It was as if Martha Stewart herself had laid down a carpet of syringes.

What astounded me most was how efficiently New Yorkers battling substance use disorder are able to compartmentalize their living situations on the basis of their habits. My first apartment after college had a similar setup. Crack in the basement, heroin on the first floor. My roommate and I were holed up in the attic, because we were the only two squares living in the building. And yet like clockwork, a steady plume of synthetic K2 smoke drifted up from the second floor.

Once again, it wasn't the first nor the last time that I wandered into a shooting gallery; but for a number of reasons, this one was easily the most impressive. First, defying all perceived wisdom about junk killing a person's sex drive, two crust punks—presumably boyfriend and girlfriend— were seriously going at it on a dingy mattress on the floor. I'm talking hot and heavy passion here: so much so that it took them a while to even notice that Matt and I had rolled up on them. Second, an equally enthusiastic crust-punk pit bull was gleefully wading through the sea of needles like it had broken into a factory of extremely sharp chew toys. Finally, above all, the place had the largest number of dirty needles I had ever seen in my life. You couldn't make a single step without hearing the snap, crackle, and pop of a syringe.

I hadn't noticed him before, so I was even more startled when a guy on the couch suddenly shot up from the dead and screamed, "What the fuck!?" It was the '80s bad-guy street punk I'd seen picking his nose with Matt outside the court. His shout disturbed whatever insane equilibrium had governed the mood of the squat. Alarmed, the pit bull abandoned its intravenous chew toys to run up barking and snarling at me. For whatever reason, a wave of modesty came over the punk nudist couple—they scrambled clumsily, diving over each other trying to cover up.

The street punk was pissed: "What the fuck, Matt? You can't just bring people in here like that!" Matt, being rather soft-spoken, was hesitant to respond, so I jumped in. I told the guy to relax, since I clearly wasn't a cop. Truth be told, heroin addicts are some of the most magnanimous and accepting people you will ever meet. With a little calm in my voice, he didn't really need much convincing to chill out.

Since this squat was where Matt actually lived, he took a load off by plopping down on an armchair. However, this unremarkable gesture made my predicament a bit tricky. The street-punk roommate, having gone from wary to hospitable, offered me a seat next to him on the couch. Now, I'm not the most well versed in the nuances of mainlining heroin, but I knew enough to recognize that sitting on the couch was the easiest way to get myself poked by a syringe. Rule number one for any drug den: never sit on any couch, unless you want to risk getting stuck in the ass by a needle hidden between the cushions.

The real issue was that I simply couldn't think of a good-enough excuse to stay standing. What was I supposed to say: "I'm good for now, but next time I'll be up to date on my hepatitis shots, so I can kick it with you on the couch and there won't be a problem"? Even now, I still don't know what would have been the most courteous way to decline the hospitality from my affable benefactor without offending him. Caught in a jam that I had no answer for, it finally dawned on me that I had landed myself in a very unsafe situation.

Still drawing a blank, I blurted out: "Oh shit, I forgot something—I actually have to go." When I say those struggling with opiate dependence are some of the most stand-up people you could ever meet, I mean it. I'll never be able to adequately convey the sincere regret in the room when I left so abruptly without properly making their acquaintance. Even the crust-punk pit bull looked bummed. And honestly, it makes sense: heroin is the preferred drug of the most sensitive and beautiful souls humanity produces; and the world always finds a way to destroy precisely what makes them so sympathetic and generous.

Given all the commotion I'd experienced ascending those Dantesque levels of controlled substances, it was almost strange how exiting the building with Matt turned out to be uneventful. Once we got outside, Matt began to apologize profusely—clearly sensing that I had been uncomfortable in the place he called home. Finally gathering my wits again, I replied, "There's no reason for you to say sorry; you didn't know I was afraid of dogs." At least it wasn't a complete lie. Along with being afraid of the dark, growing up in New York had left me with a real phobia of what was once a thug's favorite non-human companion: the pit bull. Still, I was the one who should have apologized. After all, it was his home—and deep down, I'll always believe that if it was good enough for him, it should've been good enough for me as well.

After we said our goodbyes, I gave Matt a heartfelt hug. I had a feeling that I would never see him again. Usually, I try to sidestep farewells, because I assume I'll cross paths with people somewhere down the line. But after he reminded me about his plan to sail the Pacific Ocean in a DIY boat, I knew—even if he somehow pulled it off—this was probably it. At least at the time of writing, the last I saw of Matt was a final wave goodbye that night, as I began pedaling away from the squat.

This is where the story may get a little hard to believe. All I can say is that most people—especially the ordinary American middle class—don't have the slightest clue about how wild lived reality truly is. The world is full of extraordinary people who do extraordinary things, each of which defy everyday beliefs about what is possible. New Yorkers, spending most of their lives split between the street and the subway, are continually exposed to this latent potential for the fantastic, so that the pure insanity of life can run down on them at any moment like a hungry stickup kid with their ribs touching. It made sense, then, why the Nuyorican poet Miguel Piñero was so quick to dismiss Gabriel García Márquez and Latin American magical realism: "There are no floating butterflies around my head when I walk down Avenue B, you know."[11] And who needs a butterfly, when any old-school New Yorker can tell you a story about running into angry sewer rats bigger and meaner than any rottweiler.

As I headed south on Franklin Avenue, I was obsessively examining myself to make sure I hadn't been accidentally jabbed by a needle, when this chaos started to hunt me down. It began with the sound of a faint buzz that I first heard riding past the Ol' Dirty Bastard mural on Putnam. Thinking my mind was playing tricks on me, I tried to dismiss the sound until I couldn't ignore how the initial murmur had turned into a loud screech.

Whatever the blaring noise was, I resolved to myself that I was not going to be its victim. And so I tried to outrun it by pushing faster down Franklin. Not even consuming all the performance-enhancing drugs at the Tour de France would have made a difference, because it steadily inched closer behind me.

Reaching the intersection of Franklin and Atlantic, whatever composure I had left collapsed into an emotional breakdown. In a panic, I jumped off my bike, leaped onto the sidewalk, and tried to make a run for it with my Bianchi slung over my shoulder. I headed straight into a group of older Black men congregating in a circle. Likely connoisseurs of crack or heroin, they nevertheless had a cultivated air that gave the impression of those winos of yesteryear. Donning Kangols and newsie hats, these gentlemen could have easily been extras in the video for Gil Scott-Heron's "The Bottle." Dispensing with the formalities that men of their stature require, I couldn't do any better than gasping, "What the fuck is barreling down on me?"

Having presumably held court on that exact location for decades, it was obvious that these old fellas prided themselves on having seen it all. After a glance at one another, it was as if they'd already decided whose turn it was to deliver the next explanation. So their elected representative, in the hip fedora, stepped forward and broke it down like I was born yesterday: "Look, young blood, what you're seeing is a driver who is drunk and too intoxicated to realize that their tire has been popped."

Sure enough, the horrible screeching noise I was trying so hard to escape was nothing other than metal wheels, without the prophylactic of rubber tires, grinding directly on the asphalt. "Look over there," Mr. Fedora said, as he pointed at a black SUV careering toward the intersection with its wheels spewing sparks like flamethrowers. I'd be skeptical myself if I hadn't seen it with it my own four eyes, but as dawn crept into those Brooklyn streets, I did indeed witness a truck emitting vertical streams of fire straight up into the air. Think *Mad Max*; think *Twisted Metal*; think, How is this entire night even still happening?

Before it came into focus, I already knew that the SUV would have New Jersey license plates. In the driver's seat sat a thirtysomething blonde Karen wearing the blank smile of a psycho-slasher hopped up on Thorazine, totally oblivious to the chaos she was unleashing. You could tell she fancied herself Princess Diana meets Sarah Jessica Parker—though even with such low-hanging fruit for role models, she was more like the zombiedirtbag version of both. "See, I told you so," Mr. Fedora said to me with a wry grin.

After a wide turn onto Atlantic Avenue sent sparks blazing into oncoming traffic, I felt vindicated in that the first wave of early-morning commuters seemed as scared as I was. With the sun beginning to peek out, the whole block caught a glimpse of her deranged, makeup-smeared face. I overheard someone quip, "Well, she's got a long ride back to Jersey." Likewise, I decided to take my time and walk the rest of the way back home to start working through everything I'd seen that night.

It's hard for me—or probably anyone—to extract a moral from this story. The best I can do is state what is, paradoxically, the deepest of all platitudes: "Life's ill; sometimes life might kill."[12] Since our paths never crossed again, I sometimes daydream alternative fan fictions about what might have happened to Matt. Since he was headed to the San Francisco Bay Area for his makeshift boat trip around the world, I imagined him falling in with another band of outcasts with the same travel plans. The media labeled them a cult, but I refer to these self-declared vegan anarchists as "the poor man's Luigi Mangione": the so-called Zizians. I can almost see Matt in the hull of their rickety ship during a violent storm on the Pacific, sharing his lofty ideals and harrowing experiences. After returning safely from their journey, the Zizians would translate what they heard into action by declaring war on all forms of normative coercion, while I know Matt would go with God, in another direction, to who-knows-where. But if you do know, tell him to call me.

6

Postscript: On Pain

> Since it seems that any heart which beats for freedom has the right only to a small lump of lead, I demand my share.
> —Louise Michel

After revolt has settled into the definitive past, it's hard for me to find anything worthwhile to say. In fact, at the risk of sounding melodramatic, when normality and stability once again reassert their dominance, I honestly can't see the point in doing much of anything and even the simple task of living can prove to be quite difficult. Furthermore, I would wager that each of us has had some familiarity with this condition, in which the expenditure of an effort is accompanied by some level of distress, ranging from slight discomfort to the most severe anguish.

As much as I hate to admit it, two thoroughly bourgeois academics have provided the most accurate recent description of how widespread this predicament has become:

The lives of many millions of Americans are comprised by pain; some cannot work, some cannot spend time with friends or loved ones in the way that they would like, some cannot sleep, and some cannot do the activities that make daily life possible and fulfilling. Pain can undermine appetite, induce fatigue, and inhibit healing; in extreme cases, it erodes the will to live.[1]

What's more, the authors also do well in identifying the necessary psychical and social dimensions underlying what would ostensibly appear to be a purely physical instantiation of pain:

Social and community distress, the labor market, politics, and corporate interests all collide around pain, and pain is one of the channels through which each of them affects deaths of despair. In our search for the story behind the deaths, pain kept coming up, in apparently different contexts. Pain is an important risk factor for suicide; the victim believes that the intolerable pain will never get better. The treatment of pain is a root of the opioid epidemic. The brain's natural opioid system controls both euphoria and pain relief. People use the language of pain and hurt to describe "social pain," from rejection, exclusion, or loss, and there is evidence that social pain uses some of

the same neural process that signal physical
pain, from stubbing a toe or cutting a finger, or
from arthritis. Tylenol can reduce social pain as
well as physical pain.[2]

It is now a sufficiently documented phenomenon
within the relevant literature, but for those of us
who have been through a struggle with the dark
recesses of ourselves, we've always been well
aware of the intimate and reciprocally interwoven
relationship that binds together emotional and
corporeal suffering. It routinely comes about in the
immense psychological strain that is often required
just to physically pull oneself out of bed and the
embarrassing anxiety that manifests itself as something carried deep in the intestinal tract.

On the basis of its intrinsically socio-psychical
nature, the authors derive two further consequences from their account of human hurt, pain,
and injury, both of which merit further elucidation.

First, rather than suggesting mindfulness techniques, they instead locate the root of our ongoing
epidemic of suicidal misery and homicidal rage, as
well as many of its immediate contributing factors,
firmly within the prevailing configuration of our
current social order. However, as with most of the
astute judgments that earn today's specialists the
highest scholarly accolades, Guy Debord had
already fully informed us on this matter more than

forty years ago. Meticulously cataloguing the "physical, intellectual, and psychological degeneration" of the planetary petite bourgeoisie, what Debord asserts in his 1978 film, *In Girum Imus Nocte et Consumimur Igni*, about this burgeoning salariat ("which has never been very bourgeois and which is scarcely any longer working-class") also anticipates precisely what will later be distinguished as the precipitating causes behind the increasing number of deaths of despair.[3]

Debord's diagnosis encompasses what would today be apparent to anyone brazen enough not to avert their gaze upon encountering the residents of Anytown, USA. The list includes a haggard and pallid countenance due to a qualitative decline in the commodities available for consumption: "ill-nourished with tasteless and adulterated foods" and "passively accepting the constantly increasing repugnance of the food it eats, the air it breathes and the dwellings it inhabits."[4] Consequently, they are hindered by chronic ailments, but lack health care: "poorly treated for their constantly recurring illnesses ... they die in droves on the freeways, and in each flu epidemic and each heat wave."[5] The result was what Pasolini had also long ago noticed about the undead casualties of capitalist restructuring: "there's no light in their eyes, their lineaments are like the forged lineaments of automata, they do not know how to smile or laugh."[6] In the same way that Aimé Césaire saw how Western civilization's penchant for colonial oppression and technological warfare had exposed the inherent barbarity in its half-hearted humanist project, Pasolini witnessed firsthand its overt somatic expression in how we have become, in his words, flat out, "ugly."

Above all, what Debord keenly understood, which today's pseudo-critics are only finally beginning to realize, is that this pervasive suffering is tantamount to the reduction of life to a bare, lonely, and utterly meaningless form of survival:

> Separated from each other by the general loss of any language capable of describing reality (a loss which prevents any real dialogue), separated by their relentless competition in the conspicuous consumption of nothingness and thus by the most groundless and eternally frustrated envy, they are even separated from their own children, who in previous eras were the only property of those possessing nothing. ... Understandably despising their origin, [these children] feel more like offspring of the reigning spectacle than of the particular servants of the spectacle who happen to have begotten them. ... Behind the façade of simulated rapture among these couples and their progeny there is nothing but looks of hatred.[7]

It should be noted that this characterization poses a preemptive challenge to privilege discourse, since the archetype of this depraved individual is clearly the white American citizen. If anything, Debord's primary shortcoming was that he couldn't foresee how so many would eventually opt for a suicidal retreat from this earthly hell, since the spectacle of his era was still capable of parading out its inverted utopian image of a commodity paradise. However, on today's nihilistic horizon, the only momentary illusion of a "happy, eternally present unity"[8] appears with the insertion of a syringe.

Second, the mind's promotion to the very focal point of the unfolding of pain entails its comprehensive reconceptualization. Put in another way, if its occurrence can no longer be deduced from a discernible physical injury, then pain cannot be feasibly conceived as solely a unidirectional signal relaying a cautionary message from the body to the mind. Hence, there is a growing acceptance, also endorsed by the National Pharmaceutical Council, for tautologically defining the sensation as "whatever the experiencing person says it is, existing whenever s/he says it does."[9] A welcome attribute of this formulation is that it clearly undermines the professional's haughty expertise with regard to our misery, because it emphasizes subjective awareness over any objective evaluation: "the patient, not the clinician, is the authority on the pain and … his or her self-report is the most reliable indicator."[10] Yet, besides its susceptibility to manipulation by the two-bit peddlers of oxycodone, the other major problem with such a definition is that it tends to lock each of us up, alone with our hurt, in a cage constructed of autonomous individual subjectivity. Hence, we incessantly hear statements about, "my trauma," as if it were a prized personal possession. But it is more like a solipsistic Daniel Defoe or Ibn Tufayl narrative injected with a nightmarish dose of gothic horror.

Returning to my opening remarks, this explains the futility in trying to communicate with one another in periods of deadening social peace and harmony: however eloquently it might be articulated, there nonetheless exists a reigning injunction against sharing what is undoubtedly the most profound and vital aspect of the human condition—namely, our capacity to suffer. Currently, the spontaneous ideology surrounding our hermetic confinement within ourselves has been codified under the guise of standpoint epistemology. Yet, like being caught red-handed with instruments in the furtherance of criminal activity, we are increasingly deprived of what might be needed to convey anything of substantial importance.

It should be obvious by now that only the staggering disruption brought about by revolt is equipped with the power to bring down what bars any mutual access between otherwise distinct, separate, and atomized entities. Given that pain's ineluctably social origin is prohibited from escaping the lone trappings of the afflicted individual, the dilemma can only be resolved by an equally aporetic gesture, enacted by a *universal character attained by its universal suffering, and which claims no particular right on the basis of no particular wrong, but wrong generally is perpetuated against it.* Of course, this could never be achieved through idealist methods, whether it be writing, speaking, or diversity training. Instead, like the old man once told us, *every step of real movement is more important than a dozen articles and essays.*

7

The Revolt Eclipses Whatever
the World Has to Offer

GERARDO MUÑOZ. Idris, thank you for this dialogue on the current moment in America. I suppose a pertinent starting point is the ongoing civil war. This is a problem that has been of interest to you for some time. Certainly, this civil war is not necessarily between two familial sides, as it is sometimes thought of in the political tradition. In our time, this civil war is also taking place on the plane of legality (a "superlegality," as I have recently called it), but which has all the ingredients of the stasiological form: total mobilization, fragmentation, reconfiguration and deployment of the police apparatus (armed formations, cybernetics, pedagogy), and the increasing decline of the principle of modern authority. We also seem to see before our eyes the exhaustion of constituent power and "civil society," which traditionally were the two poles for the renewal of "We the People." In other words, we are now in a moment that we could call destituent. What are the possibilities that are opening up, if, indeed, we can characterize this moment as one of ongoing destitution?

IDRIS ROBINSON. I think you are correct in characterizing the recent events in the United States in terms of civil war. Indeed, Dimitris Chatzi-vasileiadis, quite eloquently, summed up the current situation, when he wrote: "After centuries of slavery, the consciousness that a civil war has ceaselessly been taking place is again emerging massively. This was silenced as long as the one side, the tyrants, had the power to eradicate its memory. ... But the moment it takes again to the streets, all the memory, all the class history comes forth like a volcano."[1] For this reason, I greatly appreciated your theoretical intervention in *Cuarto Poder*, as I want to insist upon the need to truly think civil war, despite whatever intellectual reluctance might prevail.

Accordingly, what the classicist Nicole Loraux has convincingly demonstrated with regard to the significance of the Greek term, *stāsis*—which not only denotes civil war, but can also be understood as factional conflict, partisanship, and sedition—applies to the American experience as much as it did to the classical world's experiments in collective living. That is to say, civil war remains a constitutive element binding together the very structure of the political in the United States, and this is precisely why it is constantly subject to varying levels of repression within the country's historical consciousness. I'd even venture to say that civil war and race share the same status in America: both stand as an unapproachable and traumatic kernel that the nation must avoid for the sake of its own existence.

Moreover, I agree that there is a vital link between civil war and destituent power or potential, but I am not prepared to specify the stakes of this relation with the degree of rigor demanded by the problem. At most, I can say that my starting point begins with some of Giorgio Agamben's formulations on the topic. Accordingly, I take civil war to be a play of forces that mutually entails a politicization of the private realm and a depoliticization of the public sphere, thereby opening up a zone of indiscernibility between the *oīkos* and the *pōlis*, domestic and civic life. In the American framework, we are already beginning to see how the abolitionist overcoming of whiteness implies a fracturing of the family, since taking up the cause of Black liberation tends to correspond with forsaking the lineage of whiteness. The oft-repeated and rather banal narrative fed to us about the last civil war being a clash of "brother against brother" is beginning to acquire some historical thickness, as these conflicts are starting to play out again in the present moment, shattering the otherwise awkward silence that previously ruled over white American dinner tables. Likewise, the plantation can be understood as a household, where certain forms of libidinal violence were deployed in order to maintain compulsory labor. However, it is obvious, today, that the wider nation, as a whole, exhibits many of the relations that were formerly invested within the system of estates. Thus, it may be possible to define destituent power as that which moves to sever the relational network of familial and political bonds encompassed by the (American white supremacist) state.

In addition, I would like to point out how revealing it is to see the various expositors of Agamben's thought downplay or dissemble the conceptual centrality that he ascribes to civil war now that it has arrived on their doorsteps. In my view, their defensive abnegation is connected with a theme that Mario Tronti put forward in his 2005 essay "Toward a Critique of Political Democracy," but was also expressed in his well-known interview on the topic of destituent power:

> After all, democracy is always "democracy in America"; and the United States has always exported democracy with war. ... In fact, it is after the age of the European and world civil wars that democracy truly triumphed. And democracy was finally decisive for the victory of the West in the last war, the Cold War. Contrary to what one often hears, especially from progressive quarters, I deny that in the

current phase we are experiencing the centrality of war. It seems to me that this present emphasis on peace-war is entirely disproportionate. All the wars are taking place at the borders of empire—on its critical fault-lines, we could say—but the empire is internally living through its new peace, though I do not know if it too will last one hundred years. It is in this condition of internal peace and external war that democracy does not merely prevail, but experiences a resounding triumph.[2]

Now that the Pax Americana has come to an end and the neoliberal world order is collapsing in on itself, its fiercest critics become its most ardent defenders and dive through intellectual hoops so as to preserve their comfy armchair set right at the very heart of empire. Instead, I insist that the correct line to hold is that their chaos is our peace, their confusion is our sanity …

GM. You have touched on a lot of important elements and I am particularly interested in the way you are thinking about the question of *stāsis* as a process of incision and fragmentation (of the family bond, of the ideal of whiteness, but also of the social matrix), and obviously by saying this you implicitly allude to the age-old problem of violence. Or perhaps we could speak of a new "culture of violence." Of course, during the modern revolutionary epoch (let us say from Jacobinism to the guerrilla war of the '60s–'70s), violence was understood as a mechanism of sacrificial investment in the political subject, something that from my point of view would explain its limits and insufficiency. In other words, modern revolutionary violence would have been trapped in the sacrificial entelechy of the Christian liturgy. Now we can no longer speak of a "political vanguard," so that at this point a new form of violence can occur outside the hardening of subjectivity, that redoubt of Humanism. In your text "How It Might Should Be Done," you address this question in an original way and go so far as to speak of the tactics of the fox. The fox always knows how to generate strategies, because she knows when to retreat and when to advance. This is the movement of anabasis. I found this curious, and it is not minor that you think about it in the form of a fable. Could you say a little more about how you are thinking about this other dimension of violence?

IR. As is well known, this was a reference to Machiavelli's claim that two beasts—the lion and the fox—must reside in one and the same prince so as to secure the favor of virtue and fortune in politics.[3] On the one hand, the lion can overpower the wolf, yet carelessly stumbles in the hunter's trap; while, on the other hand, the fox is shrewd enough to avoid the trap, but will instead succumb to the wolf. From the perspective of revolutionary politics, both are demanded: the lion represents sheer force, violence, and the masses in an overwhelming swarm; whereas the fox represents subversion, as the capacity to undermine power without a frontal assault.

In my talk, I conceived of the trap as the spectacular misrepresentation of the George Floyd rebellion as a kind of peaceful nonevent. Recently, the comparisons drawn in progressive circles between the rebellion and what occurred at the Capitol Building on January 6 have become an additional recuperative feature of this discourse. In fact, I'd argue that the delusions that liberal America entertains about violence and race have reached levels that mirror the radical right's fantasies about QAnon. Altogether, I take everything that is associated with intersectionality, identity, and privilege politics as roughly the same kind of trap in the way that it impedes any meaningful change. Since these obstacles have become so pervasive, it will require all of the sly cunning of the fox to bypass them.

GM. It is clear that today the important thing is to affirm what we would call the dimension of the "evental" above forms and subjectivities. And it seems to me that this is what you allude to in your reading of the different animal instincts in politics. Perhaps only the fox can pull off a surprise event in the world. Along these lines, I'd like to raise a question that I don't think has been sufficiently explored: Does it seem to you that we can think of the eruption of revolt outside of its strictly "political" form (the insurrection, the occupation of an autonomous space), and thus as a movement to attack boredom and immobility? A fellow traveler of ours speaks of the *fiesta* (festivity) as a revolt of everyday life, closer to friendship than to a mobilization of direct political activity. Power today seeks to provoke and exhaust the body. Doesn't it seem to you that destitution is also a vital intuition, almost psychic, against the boredom of all subjection of life?

IR. In the modern history of revolt, we can locate both the sacrificial and the carnivalesque figure. For example, Saint Just and Nechayev are, clearly, embodiments of the former. Whereas the revolutionary sequence of '68, with its emphasis on the party or the festival, has given way to the dominance of the latter. I think that both have proven themselves to be deficient, as each remains trapped in a back-and-forth dialectic that ultimately leads back to the state. Their shortcomings can be made clear by way of Walter Benjamin's analysis of positive and natural law in his "Critique of Violence" essay. On the one hand, sacrifice overlooks the individual as a means toward a justified end; on the other hand, the carnival instead stresses hedonistic means to a consistent end in personal enjoyment. With both hopelessly intertwined within the juridical framework of means and ends, this century calls for a new configuration of the connection between lack, desire, and agency.

The best suggestion that I have come across has been Rodrigo Karmy Bolton's account of the figure of the martyr in his interpretation of Furio Jesi's *Spartakus: The Symbology of Revolt.* Due to his firsthand experiences in the Parisian May, Jesi himself observed what anyone who has ever been swept up in the fever of revolt can attest to: the insurgents in a rebellion enter into a new and different relationship with time. More generally, Jesi concludes that genuine revolt always provokes a suspension of historical time, such that the actors engaging in the event are unable to know or foresee its consequences. It follows that revolt necessarily involves a disruption of any rational justification that could bring means and ends together, because it is impossible for the insurgent to calculate the steps of action that might couple the former with the latter.

The paradigmatic outline of the martyr is endowed with substance through its total immersion in revolt, as the individual becomes both unwilling and unable to conceive of the ramifications of their actions outside of the present insurrectionary moment. That is, due to the excessive nature of revolt, he or she can no longer be bothered by the physical, psychological, or financial standards of well-being promoted by the status quo. As Karmy Bolton puts it, the martyr makes a wager on a surplus of life that goes beyond any subjective or objective reasons. Upon considering this wager, it becomes clear why it is a fundamental mistake to ever identify the martyr with asceticism, renunciation, and sacrifice.

Instead, Karmy Bolton explains in *Intifada*, "in daring to revolt, the risking of one's own person on the incalculable intensity of insurrection implies forging a link at the intersection between myth and political propaganda, the eternity of an immobile time and the contingency of history."[4] For this reason, I like to emphasize that, on the one hand, the religious tradition tends to understand martyrdom as a gift. For our purposes, we can think of it as surrendering something lesser for something else of an immeasurably greater value: a judgment that the implicit humanity and lived experience of revolt eclipses whatever the world has to offer. On the other hand, the martyr seeks to wholly inhabit this suspension of time, freezing the brief flash of rebellion, to thereby achieve a kind of secular immortality. In this way, the death of Rosa Luxemburg was a choice to forever remain within the truth of authentic revolt by eschewing the craven falsity of social democracy. Likewise, Michael Reinoehl took the possibilities manifested within the George Floyd rebellion as utterly superior to whatever worthless plastic insanity the United States of America peddles to its citizens.

GM. It's really moving when you talk about revolt as a force that can eclipse the world, something that raises to the starry skies an image that can never be appropriated or governed. That faraway gaze in the sky is the only one that can give us back something transformative to let us inhabit another earth. However, looking down, we see a new metamorphosis of power unfolding. Whether in the Chilean October, in the Yellow Vests, or in heterogenous insurrections throughout Latin America, we see that the metropolis today has emerged as a topology for the reproduction of "the world of life." In the United States, as we know, there appears what Phil A. Neel has called the "hinterland," a no-man's-land that, by virtue of its anomic condition, fragments the separation between the metropolis and its outside. I wanted to ask you about this: given the hegemony of the metropolis in the North American spatial organization (New York, San Francisco, Chicago, Silicon

Valley), would you be willing to concede that the metropolis is today the center from which destitution intensifies?

IR. There is much to say about that, but I'm only capable of touching on a few points. For starters, I think you are right to indicate the importance of the hinterlands, as you did in your review of Jason E. Smith's recent study,[5] and especially with regard to the past summer's uprising in the United States. I would also add that Shemon, Arturo, and Atticus's "Fire on Main Street: Small Cities in the George Floyd Uprising"[6] provides us with an illuminating analysis of this phenomenon.

As for myself, I've noticed, for some time now, this "banlieueification" of American cities. After decades of an exceedingly violent process of gentrification, I've witnessed certain trends in the displacement of family and friends. What is of the utmost significance is that this proletarianization of the periphery has left its imprint on a number of revolts which have caught my attention over the course of the last decade or so. For example, I first noticed something of a shift during the Kimani Gray uprising, since the absence of a direct subway line to the Manhattan center lent the Flatbush area of Brooklyn, where it occurred, some level of autonomy. Of course, the classic case of this was the Ferguson uprising of 2014. Yet, the impact of the suburbs and the small cities was truly on full display in last year's [2020's] hot summer.

On the flip side, American cities have almost unanimously suffered from a very acute concentration of capital, specifically in finance, insurance, and real estate. As a consequence, they have been transformed into complete cultural wastelands. This has a profound anthropological dimension, whereby the city-dwelling animal has internalized the very worst aspects of bourgeois society; its thoughts, feelings, tastes, and behaviors have become homogenous expressions of this emptiness. Its existence nevertheless invokes in the imagination certain fantasies of proletarians, from the outside, surrounding, besieging, and plundering the center of the city. We saw some of this last summer, but hopefully the George Floyd uprising was only the cinematic trailer to an upcoming feature-length film.

GM. Finally, let me end with a question about the sequence that is opening up after BLM and the insurrection over the murder of George Floyd: Is it possible to think of other discontinuous logics of this energy? Rodrigo Karmy Bolton, whom we have already mentioned, has spoken of a rhythmicity of the revolt, as a way to predict the duration of the event but not necessarily its future—that is, to think it outside a unification of the movement (hegemonic logic), or a second phase of an "institutional" type that translates as the intonation of the rhythms into a process of administration and social redistribution.[7] In my opinion, this brings to bear the question of how to free the fragments of the conflict from what I call a posthegemonic opening. In any case, how are you thinking about this problem in the face of the next phase?

IR. After Trump's ascension to the presidency in 2016, I've given up on making any forecasts. Whatever assurances that Americans had formerly believed they could hold on to should now only be mocked like Dave Chappelle and Chris Rock did on that notorious post-election episode of *Saturday Night Live*. However, on a more serious note, this unpredictable volatility indicates the conditions of the crisis and how deep they run. All I can say is that, with so much tumult under the heavens, the situation is, indeed, excellent …

8

Civilizing the American Wasteland

What happened?

Well, what had happened was …

Boom! 574 riots; 2,382 cases of looting.

On top of all of that … 97 cops cars set ablaze; 13 cops, themselves, were shot; and 9 of them Isised with hit and runs.

So, I can tell you what did not happen …

What transpired from May to June of 2020 was not a series of mostly "peaceful protests."

Nor was it initiated by some stupid white boy in a Hawaiian T-shirt.

Indeed, the fear of Black revolutionary initiative runs so deep in this country that, both liberals and conservatives, MSNBC and FOX News, are now competing to see who can devise the craziest of conspiracy theories.

All of this to simply obscure the facts about who triggered one of the largest and most widespread uprisings in American history.

James Baldwin once said, "One of the dangers of being a Black American is being schizophrenic, and I mean 'schizophrenic' in the most literal sense."

Yet, for a brief moment, a moment long enough to both literally and figuratively catch a breath, the roles were completely reversed: their confusion became our sanity, their chaos became our peace.

But most of all, amongst the mass of lonely, isolated, autonomous citizen-deputies, the undead of the American wasteland, with their incurable neuroses and deranged habits, we saw, for the first time, a slight glimpse of humanity.

It was the initiation of the Fanonian humanist project, laid out at the end of *The Wretched of the Earth*: a real civilizing mission.

But only for those who participated, on an almost spiritual level, with body and soul, in the non-movement, rather than the social movement.

Running with the field negroes who got loose: got loose on banks and got loose on parole offices.

But even I can feel the chains getting tighter; and I wonder how much longer they're gonna let me stand up here and talk this kind of shit.

That is to say, after a year of plague, unrest, and natural disaster, so much has happened, but still, so much remains the same ...

For instance, besides Black people, 99.9 percent of Americans continue to fall into two categories, which reflects the two-party system: either they are overtly racist or just narcissistic and annoying.

Far too often, it is some awful admixture of both.

When the crisis erupts, and the repressed make their return, the defense mechanisms go into full swing.

This is why the jargon of academics now sounds all the more hollow and empty.

Indeed, it seems like only Yannick Giovanni Marshall and Dr. Joy James had the courage to say what needed to be said.

Meanwhile, the rest of the Black intelligentsia went on trying to articulate their own unique mode of bourgeois suffering.

Self-obsession seems to be the best way to ignore Black agency, as they've been utterly incapable of addressing their brothers and sisters in the streets, burning and looting.

Be sure, our society still mobilizes all of its efforts to elaborately avoid the fundamental problem.

It is not about diversity and inclusion.

Nor is it about the treatment of people of color, whoever or whatever they are ...

It's the fact that Black niggas, and not BIPOCs, are locked down in prison, and mostly everyone, and likely even you yourself, at least on an unconscious level, believes that they actually belong there.

It's the fact that every other day some white boy shoots up a school or a supermarket, but nothing invokes more fear in an American's heart than a young Black man with an air freshener dangling from his rearview mirror.

9

Introduction to Mario Tronti's
"On Destituent Power"

It is with great satisfaction that I introduce to you the long-awaited English translation of Mario Tronti's 2008 interview on destituent power. In my various musings on the subject, I have quite bombastically referred to Tronti as "the cornerstone of *operaismo*," "the paragon of Italian Marxism," and even "the last living embodiment of communism itself."[1] Notwithstanding my own penchant for hyperbole, such exaggerated terms of endearment are intended to allude to the way Tronti tends, at least in some measure, to actually see himself— that is, as a man from another era, trapped in an alien and hostile age.[2]

Among the many merits of his more recent interventions, there is an underappreciated value in his willingness to acknowledge the prevailing defeat and failure that has accompanied the past five decades of neoliberal capitalism's triumph. Thus, in contrast to the empty anti-globalization slogan, Tronti ought to be credited for having had the audacity to say, "We are *not* winning," and for mustering the courage to recognize loss for what it really is. Sometimes the most radical gesture involves the simple refusal to seek a silver lining in circumstances that can breed nothing other than misery and anguish. As another Italian comrade once put it, "Marxism is not a doctrine for the understanding of revolutions, but of counterrevolutions: everyone knows how to orient themselves at the moment of victory, but few are those who know what to do when defeat arrives, becomes complicated, and persists."[3] In a similar spirit, the poet Sean Bonney convincingly argued that, however paradoxically, revolt does not necessarily coincide with that which is truly revolutionary. Whether in Italy following the Years of Lead, or in the United States after our hot pandemic summer, Bonney urges us to reject a false sense of comfort and instead furnish "powerful accounts of the painful return to capitalist business-as-usual after the intensity of social upheaval," and of the "agony of the collective 'I' gradually and painfully returning to its individuality as the uprising is defeated."[4] In short, although it may sound odd, there is an emancipatory impulse in chronicling the way counterrevolution comes to reconquer our physical and psychical being with its weapons of loneliness and melancholy. This approach was confirmed by Marx himself, when he stated in his notorious 1843 letter to Ruge that, "if I nevertheless do not despair, it is only because the desperate situation of this time fills me with hope."[5] Accordingly, we may regard Tronti's conjectures about the potential for destitution as a draft outline for the mobilization of precisely this kind of despair, a preliminary blueprint of what Walter Benjamin once called the "organization of pessimism."[6]

Among the many valuable insights contained in the interview, I wish to underscore five characteristic features that Tronti ascribes to any possible configuration of a destituent power:

1.

An exact and thorough understanding of time leads to a dual conception of humanity, since the collection of attributes ascribed earlier to the gods is attainable by means of a thorough study of oneself, and such a study is nothing other than humanity believing in humanity.
—*Velimir Khlebnikov*

Destituent power is wholly antithetical to constituent power, as it refuses to seek any political end, goal, or objective. For Tronti, the most emblematic example of a constituent politics is found in the historical workers' movement, with its principal aim of actualizing the socialist ideal. Whereas in an earlier phase of capitalist accumulation there may have been a certain strategic rationale for promoting socialism to the level of a constituent objective, the current conditions of exploitation have rendered such a political program obsolete, thereby providing the nascent justification for seeking a destituent alternative instead.[7]

In his allusions to the "coming sunrise" and a "bright future," Tronti offers a subtle nod to the enigmatic critique of the socialist utopian paradise contained in the fourth thesis of Benjamin's "On the Concept of History": "As flowers turn towards the sun, what has been strives to turn—by dint of a secret heliotropism—towards that sun which is rising in the sky of history. The historical materialism must be aware of all inconspicuous transformations."[8] The passage features two metaphorical images that had a profound significance within the German workers' movement. As announced in the first lines of the old anthem of the German Social Democratic Party, "Brüder, zur Sonne, zur Freiheit" (Brothers, to the sun, to freedom), the sun symbolizes how a politics grounded in constituent power is essentially a future-oriented politics, always looking forward to an impending goal of freedom, while the flower—specifically, the red carnation—represents the Social Democratic Party itself as it bends in the direction of a radiant victory. For Tronti and Benjamin, however, such a forward-looking gaze is the mark of the most shameful reformism. For this reason, the "secret heliotropism" mentioned in Benjamin's fourth thesis insinuates a Hegelian inversion in which the historical party would instead turn its perspective back toward "what has been" in the bygone eras of the past. Moreover, in "On the Concept of History," this backward glance is said to forge a link with a conception of the present that underlines the centrality of class struggle, such that "there is a secret agreement between past generations and the present one."[9] It is precisely and exclusively in the fight, here and now, that Tronti will locate the strength of destituent power: since capitalist realism has stripped us of any capacity to imagine a future without oppression, false promises about tomorrow are less likely to seduce us into postponing the conflict for another day.

2.

Let my wretched bones be buried / in a nameless cemetery in Sverdlovsk. / Because there my friends are lying / with their profiles in marble and roses. / On acid-blue fields of snow / they fell with lead in their skulls / these frontline soldiers of Perestroika.
—*Boris Ryzhy*

The emergence of destituent power is concomitant with the demise of the Modern Subject. This claim follows from a strange twist enacted within an all-too-familiar genealogical narrative: Tronti elevates the traditional proletarian worker above its classic role as a political subject, presenting it as the apex of subjectivity as such. Starting from the earliest stages of modernity, when speculative thought first began reflecting upon individual subjectivity as an abstract philosophical concept, he observes a historical progression that would eventually culminate with the collective, social, and political subject embodied in the class membership of the wage laborer. Yet despite its socialist veneer, the story he recounts tacitly corroborates constituent power's historical connection to the same epoch that gave rise to the bourgeois state.

The problem is not simply that constituent power has remained irrevocably tied to the Third Estate since the time of the Abbé Sieyès, but also that, even in its socialist guise, it has been emptied of its prior relevance, having proven itself to be increasingly deficient in setting forth aspirations capable of galvanizing the exploited masses. It is not by chance that the antiquated socialist ideal vanished from the popular imaginary at the very moment when the conventional worker-subject, which had been striving for its concrete materialization, also disappeared.

Given their stormy past, it is worth noting that, in his criticisms of constituent power, Tronti is certainly targeting Antonio Negri's more sophisticated and updated use of the term in his 1992 book *Il potere constituente* (*Insurgencies: Constituent Power and the Modern State*).[10] For Negri, the eclipse of the historical workers' movement inaugurated a phase of development that is only today revealing the true stature of working-class subjectivity and the strength of its constituent power. By contrast, for Tronti, the current stage of capitalist accumulation marks the terminus of a subject that would be capable of actualizing such a positive constituent project. Put differently, the two thinkers drastically differ in the way they read the terrain inaugurated by the so-called third industrial revolution.[11] The former views the deindustrialization of the labor process favorably as the recomposition of the working class into a more formidable subject, endowed with the knowledge and sociality characteristic of immaterial production. The latter regards this predicament as the extreme fragmentation and casualization of labor, which casts the wage earner into a tenuous state of precarity. What's more, if subjectivity is to be judged in terms of political agency, then by any quantitative or qualitative measure of the class struggle, the traditional working class has departed from the historical stage.[12] In its place, what remains is nothing other than the leftover casualties of "perestroika," or, in the terms of the area of autonomy, "reconstruction."

Amidst such bleak circumstances, Tronti nevertheless succeeds in finding a red thread: to sublate the outmoded working class also "means to conserve the essence of its method, the movement of its politics."[13] In the disappearance of the figure of the worker he locates an implicit dialectical inversion, one worthy of the well-known Sun Tzu aphorism: "However critical the situation and circumstances in which you find yourself, despair of nothing; it is on the occasions in which everything is to be feared that it is necessary to fear nothing." Once they have been deprived of their former subjective and constituent dimensions, the exploited and the excluded can now unleash their true and unmitigated destituent power on the current order of things. In this way, proletarians can finally gain the capacity to focus their struggle directly against the conditions of their exploitation without being misled by utopian ideological illusions.

3.

> *Comrades! / To the barricades!— / the barricades of hearts and souls. / The only true communist / is one who's burnt every bridge going back. … / Wipe everything old from your heart. / The streets are our brushes. / The squares our palettes.*
> *—Mayakovsky*

The theorization of destituent power has always been derived from the experience of concrete revolt. This has been true since its very beginning, when the term was coined by the militant research collective Colectivo Situaciones, in their analysis of the Argentinian uprising of December 2001. Likewise, Tronti also relates destituent power with concrete rebellion, but he expands its purview to encompass a wider sequence of revolts. For instance, he considers the mass uprising in Argentina in 2001, but he also includes within that lineage the counter-coup that erupted from the barrios of Caracas in 2002; the directed militancy of the black bloc in Seattle in 1999 and in Genoa in 2001; and lastly, he devotes substantial attention to the riots that shook the Parisian banlieues in 2005. From this broader perspective, he is then able to deepen the concept by distancing it further from the institutional trappings of constituent power.

In his evaluation of the rebellion in the suburbs of Paris, Tronti detects the prospect of new methods of struggle, but also admits that these outbursts of frustration still display weaknesses that are characteristic of the prevailing climate of defeat and proletarian decomposition. Indeed, in the past few years, we've become quite accustomed to witnessing uprisings wane into sudden bursts of desperation that ultimately exhaust themselves. In the same way that the large-scale socialist parties once channeled the constituent power contained within the historical workers' movement, Tronti maintains that some form of organization is required for a new destituent politics to have a comparable impact. Consequently, his repeated insistence that organization is the only ambit of power, force, and strength leads to the most crucial dilemma addressed in the interview: the paradoxical inconsistency between the masses and their organization, spontaneity and directed activity. That is, on the one hand, the rebellious nature of destituent power means that it is prone to unexpected eruptions; yet, on the other hand, calculated planning is the only option for harnessing its utmost potential. Since the burning problem of the relation of spontaneity and organization will likely be with us until a worldwide revolution fully succeeds, Tronti abstains from proposing any hasty responses, leaving the solution to await its verification in the laboratory of subversion.

4.

My name is J-A-Z-R-A / Here I'm illegal, in spite of the Left / I was born in the dusk of the West / And this evening is just splendid / For smashing fascist heads.
—Jazra Khaleed

The politics of destituent power are distinguished from the traditional constituent approach by remaining irreconcilably at odds with the pursuit of gradual reform. Once again, the historical workers' movement under the direction of socialist leadership best exhibits the path of piecemeal reforms. While professing long-term utopian ambitions, the socialist approach was, in fact, a mainly pragmatic pursuit of immediate and secondary gains like suffrage rights, wage increases, and improved living conditions. Yet, in Tronti's diagnosis, the perceived progress of step-by-step reform is nothing more than a slightly more comfortable cage that impedes the working class from reaching its revolutionary goal. What the weapons of critique expose in reformist ideology is how it operates by securing a comparatively small gain in return for a far greater and more devastating loss.

Somewhat ironically, Tronti turns back to Marx's reflections on the revolutionary wave of 1848, not only to help develop the above critique of reformism, but also to give a few brief hints about the putative character of a patently new organizational form. Above all, the immediate lesson to be gleaned from his interpretation of Marx's *The Class Struggles in France* is that a destituent power matures and further consolidates its own strength by more clearly discerning its target in its attack on the existing order. Yet, whereas counterrevolution is typically understood as an external opponent, he instead counterintuitively asserts that it is actually engendered by the revolutionary progress of the insurrectionary party. The idea can be traced back to the depiction of class conflict in his 1966 classic, *Operai e capitale* (*Workers and Capital*): whereas the bosses will attempt to envelop the exploited within the alleged objectivity of the economic sphere, the working class struggles to achieve a subjective autonomy that divides capital and labor into two antagonistic camps. Similarly, a movement today can mature into an organized destituent power only by instigating a similar fracture that brings about a distinct class enemy, and with this, a new and distinct form of counterrevolutionary enemy.

5.

> *The orange sun is rolling across the sky like a severed head, gentle light glimmers in the ravines among the clouds, the banners of the sunset are fluttering above our heads. The stench of yesterday's blood and slaughtered horses drips into the evening chill.*
> —*Isaac Babel*

The force of destituent power precipitates a rift in the order of things that results in states of exception, civil war, and ungovernability. As the hostilities between the party of insurrection and the party of order, the revolution and counterrevolution, develop and mature, Tronti envisions a transition from full-fledged civil war into a condition of absolute disorder. Implicitly objecting to Giorgio Agamben's formulations of global civil war and states of exception, Tronti argues that the recent neoliberal era has instead been typified by the stifling reign of normality. In a 2009 article, he insists that the world order is more accurately characterized by an imperial democratic stability, a Pax Americana: "Contrary to what one often hears, especially from progressive quarters, I deny that in the current phase we are experiencing the centrality of war. It seems to me that this present emphasis on peace-war is entirely disproportionate. All the wars are taking place at the borders of the empire—on its critical fault-lines, we could say—but the empire is internally living through its new peace, though I do not know if it too will last one hundred years. It is in this condition of internal peace and external war that democracy does not merely prevail, but experiences a resounding triumph."[14] The only possible means of inverting the routine functioning of global imperium is to organize a destituent power capable of producing a diametrically opposed enemy, and thereby provoking a clash so furious that it gives way to a completely unmanageable, uncontrollable, and ungovernable situation. On this account, it is by no means a coincidence—but rather a confirmation—that after three years of widespread unrest and recurrent uprisings, war is once again crashing at the gates of Europe. Nevertheless, the directive remains the same as it was when war had previously threatened to engulf the Continent: let us transform the imperialist war into a civil war!

10

The Destituent Urge Is Also a Destructive Urge: Agamben, Aristotle, and Benjamin on the Potentiality of Destitution[1]

> This is where we meet each other
> once the cameras have been destroyed,
> once the metering of time by hallways and workdays
> by which we experience a change of ownership
> has been destroyed, and the face deformed by
> things it has to say, destroyed,
> and the diagrammatic metals of combustible
> elsewheres, destroyed,
> and the destruction, destroyed.
> —Jasper Bernes, *We Are Nothing and So Can You*

Destituent power speaks to the sequence of riots, uprisings, and insurrections that we are all living today. Nevertheless, the subsequent return to normality continues to disappoint the hope that these events have managed to give to even the most cynical among us. Broaching the abstract and the concrete, the contemplative and the practical, the struggle to clarify the concept of destituent power contains within itself the possibility of a break with the current political impasse.

As is now commonly acknowledged, the militant research group Colectivo Situaciones is credited with coining the term *destituent power*. Drawing up a balance sheet of the Argentinian uprising of December 2001, the collective advanced the notion as a theoretical rendering of the revolt's most popular demand, "¡Que se vayan todos!" (All of them must go!):[2] "The sovereign and instituting powers [*potencias*] were the ones that became rebellious without *instituting* pretensions ... while exercising their *de-instituting* [*destituyentes*] powers on constituted powers."[3] In other words, Collectivo Situaciones posited the notion of destituent power to capture the Argentinian mass's insatiable drive to repeatedly topple and overthrow without seeking to replace the unseated authorities.

As is implied above, destituent power can be understood by way of contrast with earlier models that aim to institute revolutionary change on the basis of constituent power. According to Antonio Negri's expansive view of constituent power, the latter can be broadly defined as any generative, constructive, or creative power or potential.[4] In a specifically political context, this thoroughly modern conception of power is typically derived from some variation of the popular will, the people, the nation, the masses, or the multitude.[5]

Conversely, constituted power is the product or result of what a constituent power happens to construct, institute, or authorize. Accordingly, the binary coupling of constituent and constituted power will be a constantly recurring theme in what follows. As for its tangible instantiation, constituted power was initially conceived as a written constitution sanctioned by the people. However, for the present purposes, a more comprehensive list of institutions would include any established authority or normative framework, whether legal, juridical, or otherwise, or any executive or legislative governing body. In short, we may identify constituted power with any form of sovereignty or state. Note also that, for virtually every thinker discussed below, constituted power points toward a Thermidorian phase, which involves the capture and reification of emancipatory potentialities. In fact, the merits of each theoretical framework considered can be evaluated on the basis of how well it can elude, subvert, or undermine the constituted power of the state.

The Italian Marxist Mario Tronti was the next thinker to make a significant contribution to the debate.[6] As did Colectivo Situaciones, Tronti thinks destituent power through the experience of concrete revolt, but he contextualizes the events in Argentina within an ongoing periodization of social upheaval: the Los Angeles rebellion of 1991, the black bloc's directed militancy in Seattle in 1999 and in Genoa in 2001, the 2001 counter-coup from the barrios of Caracas. Yet most of his attention is devoted to the uprising that erupted in the Parisian *banlieues* in 2005. From these observations, Tronti specifies two conditions associated with destituent power, in terms opposed to its constituent antithesis: first, destituent power rejects any program that strives to obtain an objective, goal, or ideal end, whether it be a constituted power or otherwise; and second, destituent power is taken be a wholly negative and destructive capacity.

To date, the Italian philosopher Giorgio Agamben must be credited with having put forward the most sophisticated and rigorous account of destituent power, grounding it within the diverse conceptual apparatus that he has been systematically developing throughout his extended *Homo Sacer* project. More than merely pointing out all the apparent weaknesses that beset constituent politics, he relies on two theoretical schemas to demonstrate how these problems arise from an indissoluble link between constituent and constituted power. The first is Aristotle's modal ontology, as is most notably explicated in Book Theta of the *Metaphysics*. The second is the political theology that Walter Benjamin elaborates in his celebrated 1921 essay "Toward the Critique of Violence." What is perhaps even more important is that each schema can provide its own illuminating example of destituent power. In the first, a notion of destituent power arises from an encounter between Athens and Jerusalem, in which the apostle Paul's messianic visions are read through the lens of Aristotelian ontology. As for the second, it equates destituent power with Benjamin's explanation of a pure and divine violence.

Agamben undeniably lends much needed clarity and precision to the still burgeoning conversation, yet his analysis is not without its shortcomings. Contrary to what Colectivo Situaciones, Mario Tronti, and others have adduced from the current cycles of unrest,[7] Agamben rejects any paradigm of political change centered on revolt:

> And if revolutions and insurrections correspond to constituent power, that is, a violence that establishes and constitutes the new law, in order to think a destituent power we have to imagine completely other strategies, whose definition is the task of the coming politics. A power that was only just overthrown by violence will rise again in another form, in the incessant, inevitable dialectic between constituent and constituted power.[8]

By presupposing that revolt is, to some degree, responsible for the failure of constituent models of political transformation, Agamben infers that a destituent approach to politics must instead eschew these trappings in order to successfully sever itself from constituted power. As is also suggested in the above quote, his dismissal of revolt coincides with a repudiation of the tendencies for negation and destruction that had previously been detected within destituent power. More to the point, he speaks of "a destituent strategy that is neither destructive nor constituent."[9] So, instead of abolition, he often seems to suggest something of a delinking strategy, which insinuates flight, retreat, and desertion, such that a destituent power is meant to liberate itself from the web of relations that encompass constituted power.

In what follows, I argue that Agamben's strategy of destitution as desertion cannot satisfy his own self-imposed requirement of devising "a purely destituent potential [that] never resolves into a constituted power."[10] As I seek to show, to finally rid the state from the historical horizon, Agamben's proposals must also be complemented with a strategy of destitution as destruction. To preserve the valuable insights of the *Homo Sacer* project, I proceed by way of an immanent critique, to demonstrate that both Aristotle's and Benjamin's frameworks actually imply two forms of destituent power: one as desertion, the other as destruction.

Peripatetic Messianism

In Agamben's heterodox interpretation of Aristotle's modal doctrine, constituent and constituted power are respectively translated into the ontological categories of *dūnamis* and *enērgeia*.[11] On the one hand, *dūnamis* can be variously rendered as "capacity," "ability," "faculty," "power," "potential," or "potentiality." On the other hand, *enērgeia* is often rendered as either "being at work," "act," "activity," or "actuality."

As is well known, Aristotle repeatedly reminds us that potentiality or *dūnamis* can be said in many ways (*lēgetai pollachōs*).[12] Limiting its range of meanings, Agamben is primarily concerned with *dūnamis* as a specifically human potentiality.[13] In particular, he focuses on the so-called second sense of *dūnamis*,[14] due to its rank in the list of potentialities unfurled in *De Anima*.[15] In its second sense, potentiality is that which can be possessed only after learning or acquiring a certain knowledge or skill. For example, a person must first learn the construction trade in order to become a builder, but after the necessary instruction, and barring any external hindrances, the person is capable of actualizing their potential to build and thereby can erect a house.

Following Martin Heidegger's influence,[16] a pivotal stage in Agamben's interpretation is Aristotle's polemic against the Megarians, "who say that something only has potential [*duasthai*] when it is actualized [*energē*], and when it is not actualized, it has no potential."[17] For example, in the Megarian view, construction workers can maintain their capacity to build only within the very act of building, yet during their lunch break they lose this ability. However, Aristotle argues that this specious reduction of all potentiality to actuality entails "absurd consequences [*sumbaīnonta ātopa*]."[18] To begin with, not only is it implausible for workers to be deprived of their potential to build when going on break, but it will also be unclear how they could resume their activities once their break is over. Similarly, the Megarian perspective would also imply that people go blind whenever they cease to actively exercise their sense of sight.[19] Due to its preposterous consequences, Aristotle concludes, "if we cannot say this, it is clear that potentiality [*dūnamis*] and actuality [*enērgeia*] are different."[20] Accordingly, for Agamben, an adequate account of potentiality must therefore explain "the fact ... that the [builder] keeps his ability [*potenza*] to build even when he does not build," and likewise for all other *technē*.[21]

To secure the independence of potentiality, Agamben turns to a series of remarks dispersed throughout Book Theta: "Every potentiality is impotentiality [*adunamīa*] of the same and with respect to the same";[22] "What is potential can both be and not be. For the same is potential as much as with respect to being as not being."[23] That is, if potentiality is truly set apart unto itself, then one must be able to withhold its actualization. For similar reasons, Agamben designates this abstaining from act as "potentiality not-to," "capacity not-to," or simply "impotentiality." In his helpful discussion on the topic, Kevin Attell clarifies why *dūnamis* and *adunamīa* are mutually constitutive and hence coexistent:

> The potentiality not to (be or do) is, of course, absolutely essential to any potentiality. Indeed, you cannot have the latter without the former, since without the potentiality not to pass over into act, potentiality would always simply be and immediately lead to actuality; all potentialities would always be realized and the Megarians would be right. The two form an indissoluble pair and cannot be conceived independently of one another.[24]

Put succinctly, only upon acquiring a power can its activation be suppressed, and vice versa. Thus, for example, a construction worker has the potential both to build and not-to build.

The focal point of Agamben's commentary is his elucidation of potentiality's transformation into actuality, which is encapsulated in a single proposition from Book Theta: "Potential is that for which, if the actuality of which it is said to have potentiality is realized, nothing will be impotential."[25] The construction in the last clause ("*no*thing will be *im*potential") signifies a double negation of potentiality. Following the specifications in Aristotle's *De Interpretatione*,[26] Agamben maintains that this is a *privative* negation, such that the negation of the "potential-*not*-to" is not canceled out in the formulation, the "potential-*not-not*-to." That is, a self-negation within the realm of potentiality leads to actuality, in which potentiality is preserved and fulfilled in the act.

Translating this interpretation back into the domain of politics, Agamben's objection against the proponents of constituent power is that they essentially take up a Megarian position: since constituent power is generative and constructive, it is a misconception of potentiality that turns out to be indistinguishable from actuality. Furthermore, for Agamben, if constituent and constituted power are instead rendered into a proper Aristotelian modal binary of *dūnamis* and *enērgeia*, then it becomes apparent why constituent power, despite its emancipatory pretensions, always arrives back at the constituted power of the state: the former remains linked to the latter in the same way that potentiality is preserved in actuality. In speculating about how constituent and constituted power could be delinked and uncoupled, Agamben offers an early prototype of his later notion of destituent power as desertion: "One must think the existence of potentiality without any relation to Being in the form of actuality."[27]

Agamben's fully developed account of destituent power is derived from a biblical exegesis of some of the more ostensibly antinomian remarks attributed to Saint Paul.[28] In particular, he argues that the Messiah's return destitutes the constituted power of the law by specifically subduing its normative force. Put another way, it is a process that exclusively targets what the apostle from Tarsus refers to as "the law of works [*nōmos tōn ērgon*]," which strictly coincides with the legal sphere of prescription and proscription (Rom. 3:27–28).

For Agamben, the messianic transformation of the law is disclosed through his distinctive translation of the Pauline use of the Greek verb *katargēo*, "I put out of work," "I render inoperative," or "I deactivate."[29] However, he is careful to distinguish this subtle enervation of the law from its outright abolition: "The messianic is not the destruction of the law but the deactivation of the law, rendering the law inexecutable."[30] This difference is initially drawn on the basis of an etymological analysis: "*Katargēo* is a compound of *argēo,* which in turn derives from the adjective *argos,* meaning 'inactive.'

The compound therefore comes to mean 'I make inoperative, I deactivate, I suspend the efficacy.'"[31] Thus, the verb *katargeō* ("I put out of work") is said to have inherited its meaning from *argēos* ("not working," "not doing," "to idle"), which is the alpha-privative of *ērgon* ("work," "task," "action"). The analysis continues:

> This term ... does not mean "to annihilate, to destroy"—or, as one recent lexicon suggests, "to make perish ... [*katargeō* being the negative equivalent of *poiēo*]." Even the most elementary knowledge of Greek would have shown that the positive equivalent of *katargeō* is not *poiēo*, but *energeō*, "I put to work, I activate." ... The etymological opposition with *energeō* clearly demonstrates that *katargeō* signals a taking out of *energeia*, a taking out of the act.[32]

The crux of his argument is that *katargeō* does not stand in opposition to the Greek verb *poiēo*, "I make," "I create," "I produce," or "I construct." Hypothetically, if there were such a contrast, then the reversal would convey meanings deemed unacceptable, such as "I destroy," "I annihilate," or "I eliminate." Therefore, if the standard definition of *katargeō* is divided into two sets of meanings or reportative usages, as is indeed the case in most biblical lexicons, then clearly Agamben only approves of the first, "I make inoperative," and rejects the second, "I destroy."

In a more properly philosophical argument, *katārgesis* transposes the Aristotelian *dūnamis/enērgeia* dichotomy. Following Gershom Scholem's paradigm of messianic inversion, which makes "the unfulfilled fulfilled and the fulfilled unfulfilled," Agamben concludes that "here potentiality passes over into actuality and meets up with its *telos*, not in the form of force or *ergon*, but in the form of *astheneia*, weakness."[33] This reversal, rather than negation, of *enērgeia* and *ērgon* results in *asthēneia*, also "feebleness" or "lack of strength," which is a correlate of impotentiality. In this way, the reversal suggests a kind of destitution through desertion by nonagents, who hear the Messiah's call and respond by withholding the activation of their potentialities.

Likewise, destituent *katārgesis* carries out a similar inversion on the constituted power of the law: "Just as messianic power is realized and acts in the form of weakness, so too in this way does it have an effect on the sphere of the law and its works ... by de-activating them, rendering them inoperative, no-longer-at-work."[34] That is to say, the *enērgeia* inherent in earthly law, which is responsible for its binding and compulsory force, is depleted by destitution. Consequently, this deactivation also releases potentiality from the hold of actuality: "[The Messiah] makes the *nomos* no-longer-at-work and thus restores it to the state of potentiality, only in this way he represents its *telos* as both end and fulfillment."[35] The law must, therefore, endure, even after its destitution, because its latent and reversed soteriological *tēlos* is precisely what Paul judges as "holy [*ágios*]," "just [*díkaios*]" and "good [*agathós*]" (Rom. 7:12).

This line of reasoning, however, suffers from weaknesses, which initially emerge from a far too restrictive conception of *ērgon* and *enērgeia*. As for *ērgon*, it can in fact stand for more than just "work," "force," and "deed," as it can also mean the product of labor. Thus, there are instances in which it would be correct to render *ērgon* as "thing," "the result of work," or "that which is made."[36] As for *enērgeia*, Aristotle acknowledges, in the sixth chapter of Book Theta, that the word has a fairly broad meaning, since it resists being delimited by a straightforward definition (*hōron*).[37] Along these lines he states that, "things are not said in all cases to exist in actuality (*enērgeia*) in the same way."[38] So, rather than engaging in a futile effort to stipulate a definition, the Stagirite recommends that it is better to review, by way of induction (*epagogē*), the various linguistic uses of *enērgeia*.[39] As the sixth chapter comes to a close and throughout most of the eighth, Aristotle tends to distinguish different forms of activities and actualities with reference to a set of terms that indicate a teleological end, all of which can be heard with theological-messianic resonances: *tēlos*; *apeirgázomai*, to "finish off," "complete," or "bring to perfection"; *entelēcheia*, "fulfillment," "complete realization," or "accomplished"; and *ēschaton*, "last," "final," or "ultimate."[40] What is decisive for us is that Aristotle will show that there is a distinction in *enērgeia*, much like its linguist relative *ērgon*, between activities that have either a productive or an unproductive end.

Refining an argument that appears in the *Protrepticus, Eudemian Ethics*, and *Nicomachean Ethics*,[41] the philosopher discriminates between *enērgeia* by differentiating teleological ends, in a passage I will quote at length:

> For work [*ērgon*] is the end [*tēlos*], actuality [*enērgeia*] is the work. And this is why the name, "actuality" is said with respect to work and strives toward complete fulfillment [*entelēcheian*]. And since in some cases it is the use [*chrēsis*] that is the ultimate [*ēschaton*] (for example, seeing in the case of sight, and nothing comes-to-be [*gígnetai*] different from this besides that of sight); but from others something does come-to-be (for example, from the craft of building, a house, besides the act of

building). Nevertheless, the former case is no less an end, and, in the latter case, more an end than is the potentiality [*dunāmeōs*]: for the act of building is in [*ēn*] what is being built and it comes-to-be and exists [*ēsti*] simultaneously with the house. Therefore, in the cases where something different from the use is what is coming-into-being, the actuality exists in what is being created [*enērgeia ēn tō poioumēno estīn*] (for example, the act of building is in what is being built, the act of weaving is in what is being woven, and similarly in other cases, movement is in what is being moved [*kinesis ēn tō kinomenēno*]). But where there is not some other work besides actualization, the actuality is in the subject [*hupárchei*]—for example, the act of seeing is in the one who sees, the act of contemplation is in the one who contemplates.[42]

Following the terminology standardized by the Scholastics, I refer to what is outlined above as the distinction between immanent and transeunt activity.[43]

On the one hand, immanent activity empha- sizes use or *chrēsis* and is obviously favored by Agamben. In the immanent case, the use itself is the end (*tēlos*) as well as the final and ultimate (*ēschaton*) objective. Accordingly, immanent activity is an essentially unproductive act, as there is no additional coming-to-be (*gígnetai*) of a product or result beyond the active use itself. Put another way, there is no other *érgon* besides the *enérgeia* that is located wholly within the acting subject.

On the other hand, transeunt activity, which Agamben tends to downplay or overlook, emphasizes a product or result above and beyond the use. Thus, in the transeunt case, the activity is productive: a different thing comes to be from this act, which is the *télos* and *éschaton*. Accordingly, there is an additional *érgon*, which contains *enérgeia*. In Aristotle's examples of transeunt activities, building, weaving, and, more generally, moving and making can each be construed as the actualization of a corresponding potentiality in its second sense. Yet, in the transeunt cases, the *enérgeia* is in the very thing being built, wove, moved, or made.

Recalling the objection against a destructive *katárgesis*, it should be evident that an analysis of the term that considers *enérgeia* while exempting *poíesis* is only half the story. It is only in immanent cases, in which the *érgon* and *enérgeia* are strictly in the use, that the antipode of act and actuality is to deactivate and render inoperative. In transeunt cases, however, *érgon* and *enérgeia* are productive acts that entail construction, creation, or, in other words, *poíesis*. What is crucial for our considerations is that transeunt *enērgeia* is located squarely within the object that is being made. In fact, Aristotle underlines the subsumption of actuality in the constructed thing by referring to this relationship in the dative case, *ēn tō poioumēno* (in the thing being created).[44] Therefore, in transeunt cases, the equivalence among "to make" (*poieīn*), "to become" (*gīgnesthai*), and "to be" (*eīnai*) is such that the messianic reversal denoted by *katargēo* must be, without mincing words, *phtheirein*, "to destroy," "to annihilate," "to ruin." Looked at another way, if the *enērgeia* is inside the thing, then its reversal must be its coming apart.

It is not surprising that, in Book Theta, immediately after affirming the coexistence of potentiality and impotentiality, Aristotle then explicitly connects the pair with destruction: "What has the potential not-to be admits of not-being; and what admits of not-being is destructible [*phthartōn*]."[45] In other words, destruction is intrinsic to anything that could potentially exist or not exist. It follows that every coming to be that ends in an object, including those that are the actualization of the second sense of potentiality, must contain within themselves the possibility of their destruction. It also deserves mention that, in the philosophical lexicon that comprises Book Delta, Aristotle unambiguously claims that the reverse of coming to be is destruction: "Things being opposite are called contradictories and contraries ... from out and into which the ultimate extremes of becoming and destruction [*genēseis kaì phthoraì*] take place."[46]

More to the point, any ontological model that would omit the creation of objects, in which there is *ērgon* and *enērgeia* without *poíesis*, risks giving way to an absurd metaphysical picture: a caricature of a Heraclitean flux, swarming with unproductive powers and forces. Additionally, Agamben's repeated echoes of Guy Debord's indictment of the spectacle certainly demand an account of reality that admits the stable existence of objects, because spectacular reification is meant to, quite literally, transform human potentiality into actual material things.[47] Finally, the law itself should likely also have a status that is similar to that of a constructible/destructible object in order for it to serve as a basis from which its *enērgeia* could be drained out through a process of destitution. What is more, simply put, if you can drain it, then you can also break it.

In his later work, Agamben seems to have become aware of what these tensions entail for his larger *Homo Sacer* project.[48] For instance, in *The Use of Bodies*, Agamben addresses the earlier block quote so as to insist that Aristotle appraises an "excess of *energeia* over the *ergon* [as a product]," "being-at-work over the work," and "[the] primacy of operations in which nothing is produced other than the use over poetic operations."[49] However, Aristotle does not show any definitive preference for immanent or transeunt *enērgeia* in the above passage, and the instances in his corpus where he does make value judgments tend to be inconsistent with one another.

As for the messianic *katārgesis*, it should therefore be acknowledged that it could be either deactivation or destruction, depending on whether the original activity to be inverted was immanent or transeunt, unproductive or productive. Truth be told, this ambivalence better reflects the fact that the Pauline epistles were written not by a systematic theoretician but by a militant activist responding to the daily exigencies of bringing about the kingdom of god. As theologian Dale B. Martin has explained, it is likely that the radical antinomianism in Galatians was tempered in Romans due to the practical concerns of the new Jesus movement.[50] In this way, the former Epistle would therefore coincide with destitution as destruction and the latter with destitution as desertion.

Concerning Violence

In "Critique of Violence," Benjamin views violence (*Gewalt*) as preliminarily differentiated into two forms: "All violence as a means is either law-positing or law-preserving."[51] That is, on the one hand, law-positing violence is a means toward the creation and institution of a new legal order or state. Since it is constructive and generative, it corresponds precisely to that of a constituent power and is therefore also a fully Megarian potentiality. On the other hand, law-preserving violence is equivalent to constituted power and serves as a means toward upholding a prevailing legal order or state. Since the law-preserving violence of the state is a result that is distinct from the act of its creation, law-positing violence must also be deemed a transeunt productive activity.

The difference in ends notwithstanding, Benjamin deduces that "every violence as a means … itself participates in the problematic character of law as such."[52] In fact, he demonstrates that the positing and the preservation of the law merge into one another:

> For the function of violence in law-positing is twofold in the following sense: the positing of the law uses violence as a means, pursues as its end precisely *what* is to be established as law; in the moment of instating as law the end at which it aims, however, law-positing does not simply relinquish violence; rather, now in a rigorous sense and, indeed, immediately, it turns this violence into the law-positing kind by establishing not an end that would be free

of, and independent from, violence but, on the contrary, an end that, under the name of power [*Macht*], is necessarily and intimately bound up with it.[53]

This continuation of violence beyond obtaining its original end is what Benjamin calls "mythic violence."[54] As Sami Khatib observes, the two forms of violence that "mutually presuppose and deconstruct each other" are combined into "an intrinsic dialectic [that] leads into an inescapable and circular logic."[55] For Benjamin, the mythic power of the law triggers this endless back-and-forth cycle of emergence and decay, revolution and dissolution, which is identified with history itself.[56]

What Benjamin alternatively calls pure, revolutionary, or divine violence is that which contests the perpetuation of the law's mythic violence: "A new historical era is founded on breaking through this cycle that spins under the spell of mythical forms of the law, and on de-posing [*Entsetzung*, "destituting"] law ... and finally, therefore, on de-posing state violence."[57] In contrast to the two forms of legal violence, which operate as means to an end, this violence is distinguished as a pure means: "A kind of violence that definitely could not be either a justified or an unjustified means to those ends, and would, instead, relate to them not as a means at all but somehow differently."[58] As is indirectly implied by law-positing violence's Megarian disposition, pure violence, which is nevertheless a means, albeit a pure one, leans more toward act and activity than toward impotentiality and suppression. In fact, in "Critique of Violence" Benjamin refers to pure violence as an "action [*Handlung*]," a "deed [*Tat*]," "conduct [*Verhalten*]," and "exercise [*Ausübung*]" that "executes [*vollzieht*]."[59] Likewise, in an in-depth treatment of pure violence, Agamben repeatedly refers to it as either an "act [*agisce*]" or an "action [*azione*]."[60] Kant's definition of means in *Groundwork of the Metaphysics of Morals* demonstrates how intimately it is bound up with action: "What ... contains merely the ground of the possibility of an action [*Handlung*] the effect of which is an end is called a means [*Mittel*]."[61] Indeed, it is so hard to conceive of a means without action that Benjamin goes as far as to even include the "omission of action [*Unterlasung von Handlungen*]" within the realm of means.[62] The difference between legal means having an effect and how pure means simply affects can be exemplified in Georges Sorel's distinction between the two forms of strikes: on the one hand, the political strike is a law-positing violence that can cause, induce, or occasion (*veranlaßt*) a reform as its end; on other hand, a proletarian general strike is a pure violence that simply can execute, consummate, or realize (*vollzieht*).[63]

Agamben's strongest argument for a pure violence without destruction is derived from Benjamin's scattered remarks on purity (*Reinheit*) in the latter's notes and correspondence: "Purity ... is not a substantial characteristic belonging to the violent action itself. ... The difference between pure violence and mytho-juridical violence does not lie in the violence itself, but in its relation to something external."[64] Presuming a link between pure violence and something other, he then concludes that "even the criterion of the 'purity' of violence will therefore lie in its relation to the law."[65] It follows, given the supposed enduring connection between pure violence and the law, that the former obviously cannot destroy the latter. Instead, the law survives its destitution by undergoing veritably the same process that drained the law of its *enērgeia*: "Pure violence exposes and severs the nexus between law and violence."[66] Also, Agamben asserts that, similar to how the deactivated law became holy, just, and good, pure violence opens up "another use of the law," which is again considered its "fulfillment."[67]

Given the vast primary textual evidence that speaks to the contrary, it is difficult to accept any interpretation of the "Critique of Violence" that denies that pure violence somehow encompasses destruction, annihilation, or revolt. Indeed, if we follow the letter of the text, everything points toward a characterization of its author as a fervent partisan of revolutionary destruction. Consider, for example, what Benjamin says about the proletarian general strike, which he unequivocally identifies with its capacity for destruction: "The proletarian general strike sets itself the sole task of annihilating [*Vernichtung*] state power [*Staatsgewalt*]."[68] More verification can be found in Benjamin's translation of Sorel's use of the French *supprimer* with the German *aufheben*: "This general strike clearly announces its indifference toward material gain through conquest by declaring its intention to abolish [*supprimer/aufheben*] the state."[69] Finally, the proletarian strike is referred to as an "upheaval [*Umstrurz*]," which is categorized as both "anarchistic [*anarchistisch*]" and "genuinely revolutionary [*echt revolutionäre*]."[70]

So as to preempt accusations of pedantry, it is worthwhile to underscore how destruction, in the "Critique of Violence," is assigned a crucial theoretical function that marks a distinction between impure mythical violence and pure divine violence. On the one hand, two of the main examples of mythic violence do not amount to destruction, because their impurity is tantamount to a restraint that holds back destruction from achieving a totalizing scope. The first example is the Greek myth that recounts how the pagan gods punished Niobe for her hubris by killing her children, but nevertheless, she is spared from death to instead be left, cast in stone, on Mount Sipylus. In Benjamin's interpretation of the myth, he concludes that "this violence is not actually destructive [*zerstörend*]," because it stops short of fully erasing Niobe's presence.[71] The second, more realistic example considers a war for territory, in which the victory of one side of the belligerents is absolute, yet despite the complete dominance of one over the other, both the conquerors and the conquered take part in a peace treaty.[72] Given that the losing party's survival is a necessary condition for both factions to engage in a mutual agreement, Benjamin will therefore categorize such cases of warfare and reconciliation as instances of mythic violence, because "the adversary is not utterly annihilated [*schlechterdings vernichtet*]."[73]

On the other hand, in the biblical example of divine violence, the wrath exhibited by the monotheistic god indeed measures up to destruction, because it attains an exhaustive completeness of which no one is exempt. This all-encompassing level of destruction is illustrated by Benjamin in his telling of the story of "God's judgment on Korah's horde" from Numbers 16: "The judgment strikes privileged ones, Levites; it strikes them unannounced, without threat, and does not stop short of annihilation [*Vernitchtung*]."[74] Peter Fenves articulates what is distinct about divine violence in his introduction to the "Critique of Violence": "The site of devastation is erased too and thus, in its own way, devastated too. ... After the earth opens up and swallows Korah, not only is there no earthly or heavenly trace of this event, there is no ceremonial commemoration either."[75] A decade later, Benjamin returns to how this self-consuming violence is so absolute that it even destroys itself, when he writes that "the destructive character obliterates even the traces of destruction."[76]

Benjamin's reason for distinguishing mythico-legal violence on account of its lack of destructive capacities is a reciprocal demand for the constituted power of the law to maintain a certain twofold material stratification of secular reality: on the one side, there exists the sheer objectification of the law as power (*Macht*); on the other side, this power must always leave behind some remainder, "as an eternal, mute bearer of guilt," to assert its dominance over.[77] In a highly condensed argument, Benjamin demonstrates that this dual reification, as opposed to complete annihilation, is essential to the mythic character of the law.

The line of reasoning begins with the recognition that the conflation of law positing and law preserving into a mythic violence involves a problematization of the relation between means and ends, because there is a sustained violence even after the perceived objectives have been accomplished.

Since mythic violence can no longer serve as a "means to a predetermined end," Benjamin will then designate it as a kind of "non-mediate [*nicht mittelbare*]" or "immediate [*unmittelbare*]" violence.[78] He asks the reader to consider a temper tantrum as a simple example of a nonmediate violence: because it is an immediate expression of anger with no identifiable goal, it serves no purpose other than indicating that anger. In other words, an act of rage (*Zorn*) reinforces itself as its own end.

Benjamin also uses *manifestation (Manifestation)* as a technical term for a nonmediate violence that reflexively exhibits itself: "In its archetypal form, mythic violence is a manifestation of the gods. Not a means to their end, scarcely even a manifestation of their will, but in the first instance a manifestation of their own existence."[79] Eli Friedlander frames this self-emphasis by the gods in the pantheon as "a manifestation of force [that] is the intensification of its very identity in experience [and] its very existence."[80] What's more, Benjamin's foregrounding of mythic manifestation is what lies behind his deeper alternative reading of the Niobe story, "[the pagan gods'] violence establishes a law far more than it punishes the transgressions of an existing one."[81] That is to say, their wrath and vengeance are not a means toward correcting Niobe's behavior as its end but instead the immediate consolidation of their rule over mortals.

Removed entirely from the sphere of means, it is no overstatement to categorize mythic violence as an impure end in itself. This explains Benjamin's paradoxical formulation of the law as a violence to preserve its own violence: "Mythic violence is blood-violence over [*über*] mere life for the sake of violence."[82] Looked at another way, mythic violence comes to demonstrate itself as a reified object, in the form of power, by continually realizing its own existence as its end.

As is implicit in the relation of mythic violence over (*über*) mere life, the objectification of power imposes a two-tiered division that solidifies the "domination of the law over the living [*Herrschaft des Rechtes über den Lebendigen*]."[83] It follows that the law, as power, seeks to uphold itself in a specifically hierarchical and authoritarian existence. As Friedlander clarifies, "[Mythic violence] shows itself as that which is over and above everything else. In showing itself, it proves its authority. Its manifestation is a mark of *distinction*, it marks the very distinction of the unlimited from the finite."[84] This dual reification of unlimited power, on the one side, and a finite and guilty victim, on the other, is what is at the heart of Benjamin's interpretation of the Niobe myth: "As a stone marking the border [*Grenze*] between human beings and gods, a life [is] now more inculpated than before."[85] Gil Anidjar is therefore right to regard the attachment of blood to mythic violence as a symbolization of this division by permanently branding the condemned with an "indelible, bloody mark (Gr. *stigma*, pl., *stigmata*)."[86] What the two examples are meant to illustrate is how mythic violence perpetuates itself by setting itself over and above those who are forever blameworthy.

Upon considering Benjamin's account of the law as mythic violence, it is now possible to show that the upshot of his analysis, for a number of reasons, can only point toward the destruction of such a constituted power. The first is gestured at by the fact that law-positing violence, as transeunt productive activity, creates the law as an outcome other than itself. As was demonstrated in the previous section, the reversal of such an act of creation would therefore entail an opposing act of destruction. In fact, this is precisely how Benjamin situates this contrast: "If mythic violence is law-positing, divine violence is law-annihilating [*rechtsvernichtend*]."[87] Second, since the very essence of the created law is its existence as a reified object, a pure violence that destitutes by merely draining the force, violence, or *enērgeia* from the law would fail to alter its fundamental character as a thing. Consequently, the only real transformation that can be provoked in the law is that which rids it of its existence. Third, given that the law is an innately violent and authoritarian power standing over the guilty, it is doubtful that anything holy, just, or good could be retrieved from something so intrinsically repressive. Since there is nothing in mythic violence worth salvaging, its objective manifestation, along with its correlated hierarchical partition, is allocated for destruction by pure violence: "If the former establishes boundaries, the latter boundlessly annihilates [*vernichtet*] them."[88]

Indeed, for Benjamin, "divine violence designates in all respects an antithesis to mythic violence."[89] So, according to this opposition, if law is the mythic positing of an impure and substantial existence, then its antithesis must be its pure elimination. In a preliminary study for the "Critique of Violence," a fragment titled "World and Time," Benjamin repeatedly underlines precisely this aspect of destructive negativity:

> The principle is here: genuine divine violence can manifest itself other than destructively [zerstörend] only in the coming world (of fulfillment). Where, by contrast, divine violence enters into the earthly world, it breathes destruction [*Zerstörung*]. ... The divine manifests itself only in revolutionary violence [*revolutionären Gewalt*]. ... (In this world, divine violence is higher than divine nonviolence; in the coming world, divine nonviolence is higher than divine violence).[90]

That is, if a pure, revolutionary, or divine violence is a pure means that simply acts and affects, then it must be thoroughgoing in its destruction so as to ensure that nothing is left behind that could reassemble itself into an impure constituted power. Furthermore, if the purity of such a violence does happen to necessitate that it stand in relation to something other than itself, then the latter is a wholly transcendent thing, which is referred to above as the "coming world of fulfillment." In a few brief and passing moments in the "Critique of Violence," Benjamin denotes this otherworldly relatum as "justice [*Gerechtigkeit*]" itself, which contradicts law and is identified with nothing other than "God [*Gott*]."[91]

As with the messianic *katārgesis*, applying something like a Platonic method of definition by division to the cluster of uses surrounding the Latin term *destituo* reveals two strikingly similar collections of related significations. What is all the more interesting is that each reflects how a destituent power can relate to a constituted authority. On the one hand, the first grouping, to "leave," "give up," "forsake," or "abandon," suggests destitution as desertion: a line of flight that evades the reach of authority. On the other hand, the second, to "deprive," "rob," "suppress," "void," "delete," "eliminate," "cancel," or "abolish," instead intimates a more confrontational act of destitution as destruction.

Over the past few decades, these two forms of destituent power have coincided with two increasingly prevalent kinds of social upheavals. Let us consider how this unfolds in the American context. On the one hand, destitution as desertion was best exemplified by the Occupy movement. Indeed, the nonevents of 2011 can easily be read as a spontaneous mass attempt to escape the reified constituted powers that suffocate American middle-class life. Yet what is truly startling is that these protests tended to amount to nothing more than exhibiting the bare fact of human existence: standing in a city plaza, abstaining from action, the participants became the very expression of impotentiality and self-deactivation by simply being-there. Likewise, the drawn-out assemblies, which never seemed to reach a practicable decision, cry out to be interpreted as a collective exercise in verifying that the interlocutors have retained their human faculty for language, but as a pure means without content. On the other hand, the nationwide revolts sparked in Ferguson in 2014 and again in Minneapolis in 2020 were practical demonstrations of destitution as destruction. It is not hard to interpret these events as a twenty-first-century rendition of Sorel and Benjamin's proletarian general strike. Refusing all channels for mediation and reform, this combative mode of destituent power was the active negation of the constituted power of the state in its various guises.

Playing out side by side, yet at different spatial and temporal proximities to each other, this bipartite destitution can be observed in a host of other contexts. In the 1989 Tiananmen Square protests, student civil disobedience marked the earliest incarnation of a string of color revolutions, yet their passive resistance occurred only a stone's throw away from the clashes between the Beijing Workers' Autonomous Federation and the Chinese "People's" Liberation Army.[92] During the Egyptian Arab Spring, crowds gathered in Cairo's Tahrir Square, in a way that frequently draws comparison to the subsequent movement of the squares and Occupy, whereas farther to the north the militant soccer fans of Port Said took a more active and antagonistic approach.[93] Throughout the 2000s in France, a call-and-response dynamic set in between waves of student protest and the torching of cars in the *banlieues*. Finally, in Myanmar, ongoing repression has led to the non-action of silent protests in the cities, while the Burmese youth continue to flock to the jungle outskirts to receive training from the Karen people's armed formations.

As simple as Black and white in the United States, these observations about the dual form of destituent power show that each corresponds to society's division between the included and the excluded. Much like Guy Debord's description of the spectacular salariat in his 1978 film *In Girum Imus Nocte et Consumimur Igni*,[94] the characteristic behavior of the included yet disaffected tends to resemble Agamben's figurations of Bartleby and the Muselmann, and yet, as for the story of the excluded, it remains largely unwritten. However, as both Agamben and I have argued, what is certain is that the state's deployment of identity is what, for now, keeps them separated.[95] Therefore, it will be in the overcoming of this caesura that we will witness a power that is neither of the state nor its postmodern dispersal but is instead destituent.

11

Figs on God's Mountain

Boom, so I'm in the Holy Land for the very first time: the smell of frankincense and sheesha in the air mingles with the taste of dates; and everywhere, those brown shelved hills with little green sprouts. Jesus was out here spinning the yard. Not that soft, white, poisonous Jesus, but that feet-like-bronze, hair-like-wool Jesus: the live temple-market bum-rusher. The Prophet was also out here, but it's all the more impressive, because he arrived without having to once pound the pavement.

I'm sitting in the communal room of a hostel in the putative capital city. I'm justifiably tired, but mostly stressed, because in this part of the world, border crossings are so unnerving they make a body cavity search feel like a handshake. Suddenly, my man Barry walks in, grinning from ear to ear, telling me that he's found someone who can point us to the riot.

Now the kind of guy he brought in probably only exists in New York, LA, or perhaps Paris, but they're always transplants. They have this thing going on where they try to dress so arty that they end up looking like a wizard mixed with an astronaut. In short, what you get is Peter Pan in a black cape with a bunch of silver jewelry: a complete fucking doofus.

After I greeted the art wizard with a humble smile, this cat arrogantly strode up to me, chest popped out, to ask, "Where are you from?" That ended my nice-guy act, and so instead the entire Wu-Tang Clan jumped through my voice box as I responded: "New York. Where the fuck you from?" "I'm from Kentucky …" he answered, immediately deflated.

Sensing the tension, Barry stepped in to redirect the conversation back to the more pressing issue of where to shoot slingshots and burn tires. I suggested that we take a little walk to discuss the plan without any prying ears around. It was 2 a.m.: the winding and nameless streets of the de facto administrative capital were silent and empty in a way I'd only seen captured in a Shabjdeed video.

To break the ice, I offered the wizard a cigarette. Now, dig this: this motherfucker goes ahead, reaches into my pack, and tells me, "I'm going to take two." Never before nor after has anyone ever been this instantaneously and overtly disrespectful to me. As any Black man in America can tell you, each of us, individually, has suffered enough insults to fill up a book the length of *War and Peace*. However, this guy still wins the fucking prize for being the worst—and even writing about this, years later, the whole thing still gets me really tight.

Since my entire existence in that period of my life was devoted to finding the next riot, I somehow managed to suppress the burning anger that was overwhelming me in order to listen to what the art wizard had to say. As the guy went on and on, it quickly became apparent that he wouldn't know a riot if it had burned down his own parents' house. In fact, from the way he was talking, I concluded that he'd likely never been in any kind of protest, peaceful or otherwise. To this day, I suspect that he'd even be scared to engage in the most benign forms of civil disobedience—I mean it, a consumer boycott would have easily been too much for him. Nevertheless, his complete ignorance didn't stop him from lecturing us about the deep connections he had with "the most militant of resistance fighters."

Trying to be tactful, I was doing my best to explain to Barry that we should split, while attempting to avoid saying outright that this guy he had found was an idiot. But I got to give it to Barry—if anything, he's persistent. He kept asking the wizard questions, even though the latter's answers somehow became more and more nonsensical. Eventually, Barry inquired about the riot cops firing on demonstrations. Exasperated, I chimed in like a smart-ass: "I'm pretty sure guns work the same in every country: the people in the front get shot."

Now this is where things go left … It wasn't that the art wizard didn't appreciate my quip, but he was more upset that I spoke at all, especially when he was holding court. He turned to me, now smoking the second cigarette, and said, "You don't know anything and you sound really stupid right now!" Frankly, I remember being more outraged by his enjoying the extra cigarette at my expense than by what he actually said. Either way, I'd had about enough. There are these times when a person gets so mad that their mind goes blank and the pent-up fury itself takes full control. I had reached that point when I pulled my hand back and slapped the smoke right out of his mouth before I had the chance to think twice about it.

For a brief moment, we stood there, looking at one another, stunned, but for drastically different reasons. On the one hand, the shock written all over his face was the kind of expression specific to white boys who learn that there can actually be consequences for what they say or do. Whereas I, on the other hand, was surprised that I was slick enough to send the cigarette flying from his lips without ever touching his ugly-ass face. Once we both finally came to our senses, he let out a blood-curdling scream and rushed at me with his hands frantically flailing over his head, like a toddler on a playground or a weaker, white version of Deontay Wilder. In the same split second, I crouched slightly and turned away from him to avoid the direct impact of his tackle.

Let me stop here: I'm not trying to make this come off like I was John Wick or something. However, for some time, I had been, on and off, training in martial arts, so as to help me emotionally get over an unfortunate sequence of events, a few years back, where I was held up at gunpoint twice in the course of a month—which is a story in itself, but for another time. Due to the constraints of time and mostly money, I had never been much of a consistent student. Furthermore, I worked hard to keep up a very strict diet, such that whenever I could afford a wholesome meal, I invariably spent it all on cigarettes. Therefore, believe me when I say that I was just as astonished as everyone else there when my instinct to cower in fear somehow launched my opponent into the air, so that all I saw was just little wizard tights and little wizard shoes flying over my head. Boom! For some unknown reason, the stars must have suddenly aligned in my favor, because I hit him with a perfectly executed judo shoulder throw. The technical term for this a *seoi-nage*; but growing up in New York, any technique this devastating was fondly referred to as an "earth slam."

I was, of course, extremely proud of myself, yet my conceit was tempered by the fear that maybe the collision with the concrete had killed him. Nevertheless, it turned out that the art wizard was physically OK enough to start uncontrollably blabbering and floundering on the ground in an effort to get back on his feet. After dropping down and pinning him to the cement, I tried to reason with him: "Look, I really didn't mean to do that to you, so let's just call it over and go home." Even though I was feigning compassion for my fellow man, the honest truth was that I wanted to put an end to the situation because I was already out of breath from all the chain-smoking. As I lifted myself to let him up, the art wizard exhibited an utter lack of coordination in his effort to lunge at me from all fours. Lucky for me, his lordotic rump was in the perfect position to catch the check of my Nikes.

By now Barry was rightfully freaking out: "There's one army, two different police forces, and three different secret security agencies on patrol here; and they are all going to come together to bury us under the jail!" Despite the clear and present danger from these combined forces of repression, I'm not going to front that I wasn't starting to feel myself. Since I had landed techniques that I was never able to perform in the gym, I figured that I might as well go all out into unadulterated WWE mode. In other words, I started trying to hit the wizard with all kinds of German suplexes and powerbombs. Still, even if I knew how to pull these moves off, it was nevertheless pointless, because my smoker's cough had finally developed into a full-blown asthma attack.

While I struggled to gasp for air, Barry reminded me again that we really needed to leave. Finally gathering some situational awareness, I looked around to see a line of taxi drivers who had gotten out of their cabs to laugh together at the comedy. Also, if you consider how quiet a city with a significant Muslim population is right before the *fajr adhān*, the first prayer call, then you can get an idea of how each of the wizard's shouts managed to echo down every alley and every boulevard. Later, I'd hear others say that they thought they were hearing a late-night raid that had erupted into a gun battle. However, since he was still hurling obscenities while we managed to slink away, the good inhabitants of God's Hill were only being woken up by the art wizard's big mouth.

The purpose of this story is to shine some light on a revealing yet lesser-known sociocultural phenomenon: white people really tend to act a fool when they visit the Holy Land. Whether from Europe or North America, they always figure out some way to show their ass. Lest you think that it's just my individual bad luck, I've actually asked quite a few Black comrades who've themselves done the pilgrimage, and they have similar stories—sans the fistfight with a wizard, of course.

A good example of what I'm trying to get at is evinced in what happened when Barry and I finally found our first riot. When the protest hit the line of cops and soldiers, the white people simultaneously retreated to a safe distance, while young Brown kids half their age charged the enemy with nothing more than stones. And once the live ammunition started rattling, this implicit division between light and dark, safety and risk, amounted to an explicit assertion: our lives are worth more than theirs. Gone was the bravery of Rachel Corrie and Tristan Anderson; and what was left were merely passive and idle spectators.

It is well known that the English term "martyr" derives from the Greek *mártus*, which like the Arabic *shahīd* means "witness." And so what the uninvolved and inactive onlookers clearly demonstrated is the falsity of an attempt to bear witness without achieving martyrdom. In other words, true testimony about colonial occupation and the stakes of the fight against such oppression requires an intimate engagement that places the witness, both literally and figuratively, on the front line of the struggle. A person must therefore be willing to face both the negative and positive consequences of their participation: to endure the suffering, pain, and even death brought on by state repression, while savoring the bonds of solidarity and the profound euphoria that accompany liberation. The difficult choice faced by the martyr is that it is impossible to indulge in the latter without at least sometimes bearing the hardships of the former.

Like they're taking a therapeutic visit to the Dead Sea, white leftists and progressives often venture to the Land of Milk and Honey to purify themselves of colonial guilt. They are typically not at all conscious of this, but their wish is to experience the fellowship of struggle yet without any threat to the paltry status they enjoy due their own mother country's legacy of domestic apartheid and foreign imperialism. What they fail to realize is that the alienation they are seeking to escape is a product of the same oppression they refuse to challenge at home. Therefore, put simply, it makes no sense to go overseas, when you haven't stepped one foot across the streets into the projects. What's more, a brief vacation can't put you in the camp of decolonization, when every other day you are cozying up with the other colonizers.

Be sure, I'm not advocating for a kind of crass provincialism that recognizes no value beyond engagement in a local context. The trip itself is bound to be instructive, given that there's so much to learn from directly observing the most innovative insurgency and counterinsurgency face off with one another. However, the issue I'm diagnosing here begins with putatively adopting the stance of an objective observer and thereby declining to wholeheartedly pick a side. It's the same posture of pseudo-neutrality that leads the crisis collector to forget to apply the lessons they've learned once they've returned from overseas.

Against his assimilation into contemporary privilege ideology, it is worthwhile to remember that Aimé Césaire is unambiguously explicit about the damage that colonialism does to both sides of the division it maintains between the colonizer and the colonized:

> Come now! The Indians massacred, the Moslem world drained of itself, the Chinese world defiled and perverted for a good century; the Negro world disqualified; mighty voices stilled forever; homes scattered to the wind; all this wreckage; all this waste, humanity reduced to a monologue, and you think all that does not have a price? The truth is that this policy *cannot but bring about the ruin of Europe itself,* and that Europe, if it is not careful, will perish from the void it has created around itself.
>
> They thought they were only slaughtering Indians, or Hindus, or South Sea Islanders, or Africans. They have in fact overthrown, one after another, the ramparts behind which

European civilization could have developed freely.[1]

What these pale-faced pilgrims are fleeing from with their trips to the Holy Land is the same rot noticed by Césaire, which has now sunken to depths so abysmal that it has become abundantly apparent to everyone. Yet the possibility of a temporary physical escape cannot bring even the slightest respite from such a deep-seated ethico-psychological problem.

It is likewise no coincidence that these same tourists often make their journey at the invitation of some humanitarian organization. On a broad and collective scale, their individual dilemma is mirrored in Western humanitarianism's chronic inability to respond to the crises left behind in its former colonies by any means other than a nefarious combination of aid, dependency, and, above all, militarized police repression.[2] For this reason, whenever the struggle against occupation is at its lowest ebb and the NGO-industrial complex asserts itself, a palpable sense of corruption saturates the Terra Sancta as if a transcribed medieval travel diary had somehow become the backdrop for a gritty noir novel.

It was Césaire's prized student, Frantz Fanon, who would follow this line of reasoning to its fundamental conclusion by insisting that decolonial revolution had to nullify both sides of the colonizer/colonized dichotomy: "After the struggle, there is not only the disappearance of colonialism but also the disappearance of the colonized."[3] As for what is left in its wake, the pupil elaborates on his teacher's proposal for, finally, "a humanism made to the measure of the world":[4]

> This new humanity cannot but define a new humanism both for itself and for others. This new humanism is prefigured in the objectives and methods of struggle. ... The value of this type of conflict is that it creates the maximum conditions for cultural development and invention.[5]

Putting a torch to the smallpox blanket of humanitarianism, it is instead a new humanism in which the native will, at last, civilize the settler.

12

At the Encampments

I've always wanted to talk about this, because it means so much to me. However, since it is always such a fraught topic, I've always hesitated. This protest today, I think, is a great reason to finally share my thoughts and feelings.

So I've been to the Holy Land twice: once in the winter of 2015; and this past summer in 2023. Even though neither side of the fence is anything like the United States, what goes on there is intimately connected with this country's imperialist, white supremacist project. This is why it's so important you are all out here, because the investments of this university enable bombs to be dropped on the innocent thousands of miles away. What is happening over there is but another chapter in America's genocidal settler-colonial project. Even though it may seem very far removed, it is violence with a United States stamp on it.

Whenever the opportunity arises, I tell people that I've never been treated better than when I was on the river's side of the wall. I think it is the only time in my life when I've been treated kindly on a mass scale. Typically, I always keep my guard up, cautiously anticipating to unexpectedly get hit by the soul-crushing impact of racism. Throughout my entire life in the States, I have had to constantly worry. If I walk into a store, is the manager following me around? Has he already called the police? Did this person just call me out of my name? However, this was the only time that I ever felt perfectly at home no matter where I went.

For example, instead of someone giving me a suspicious look when I walked by or locking their car doors, literal strangers walked up to me on the street, without knowing a word of English, and out of nowhere, gave me a hug. I'd be walking down the street and someone would honk; so I'd worry if I was too flagrantly jaywalking or something. But no, they would instead lean out of their car window just to welcome me. Everywhere I happened to randomly stroll, I received real and genuine smiles.

There's a story where the great Polish comrade writer and journalist Ryszard Kapuściński talks about getting on an elevator with a guerrilla on leave, when all of a sudden, the comrade pulls out an apple and hands it to him. Similarly, on my first walk around the block in the city of God's Mountain, someone reached out and just handed me a fig, as if he knew that I attached an extraordinary significance to this quintessentially Mediterranean fruit. It wasn't a coincidence, but rather a well-established custom to make acquaintances by offering a piece of fruit to a person you've just met. As Kapuściński eloquently puts it, since fruit is these magnificent people's largest and only natural wealth, "to give someone fruit is to give him everything you have."[1] Somehow, this says everything you need to know about how wonderful they are.

Accordingly, I always say that they are the nicest people I have ever met on all of the four continents to which I have traveled. And this is why I always wanted to talk about it, because I owe it to them for how they treated me there. To describe a group as "nice" or "kind" may sound apolitical, but it is the deepest thing in the world for a people not to see color in ways similar to anywhere else I have been. It calls to mind Assata's observations about the hospitality of Cuban people in the postscript of her book.[2] In the same way, Miles Davis noticed a difference in his band when they toured overseas, because the weight of racism was taken off their shoulders. I always wished I could bring my family with me, especially my mother, so they could experience life without that persistent burden.

Whenever I happened to stumble upon a white European or American visiting, however, I would always get a huge reality check. Oddly enough, when they see you there, they hate you more and will express that hatred more aggressively than when they see you in the States. I've asked other Black people who've been there about this and they've all had similar experiences. There is a peculiar disdain, as if our Black faces manage to somehow wake up these white visitors from a pleasant dream we are spoiling. Moreover, if the interaction occurs within the context of a group, then you quickly get the feeling that the white person just wants you to leave, because your presence is ruining their predetermined fantasy of how their imagined interaction was supposed to go with their exoticized version of the oppressed.

What I came to conclude was that their problem was that these white travelers were on a journey to try to absolve themselves of their sins from back home. The color of my skin reminded them of precisely what they were trying to escape in their country of origin. Specifically, a Black face unconsciously reminded them of historical injustices that they benefited from every day. They'd gone elsewhere to forget this and to instead lay the blame on another system, which upholds a more overt apartheid of the form that has now been outlawed in the States.

On the flip side, so many of those living under occupation wanted to discuss the Black struggle in connection with their own. They would ask me about the relevance of works by Frantz Fanon and the words of Malcolm X for the Black struggle in the States today. They had kept up with the news of the police murders of unarmed Black people in America.

The protests today demonstrate the exact opposite approach to the form of whiteness implicit in the activist tourism that I'm ridiculing. Each of you, in your own way, is confronting the ongoing historical injustice that is right in front of you by refusing to shift it somewhere distant and overseas. It is not just courageous, it is right; since what is truly right always demands bravery and courage. So, just for being out here, I want to give each and every one of you your props.

The various experiences that I had within the '48 borders were much different. Back in 2015 to 2016, I had already begun to notice the creeping fascism within its society. By the time I visited again in 2023, this far-right drift had become a full-blown issue. Case in point, I was there for several of the protests against the authoritarian takeover of the judiciary. I witnessed the hostile fascists waiting on the sidelines, ready to rip signs and placards from the hands of liberal protestors.

Once again, Assata's observations come to mind. She insists that it makes a huge difference whether or not ethno-nationalism has been enshrined into state law.[3] In this regard, the fascist problem within the '48 borders stems from how the occupation has so blatantly denied others their rights. The problem is captured by the old adage, which Malcolm X made so prevalent, of the chickens coming home to roost. That is to say, the authoritarian and repressive practices imposed on the excluded Other later return upon formerly protected citizens. I suspect that if the protests become more radical, and let me underline "if," then this close association between internal and external dictatorial practices will become more apparent.

The United States is experiencing a similar dynamic. In the past ten years or so, this country has had its own return of fascism and authoritarianism. I call it a "return," because a key tenet of its imperial policy was to externally export and impose fascism worldwide. Post-war United States foreign policy provides us with dozens of examples of this. In Latin America, the United States engineered the coup in Chile that would install Pinochet. In Asia, the United States provided unwavering support for brutal and bloodthirsty fascists like Chiang Kai-shek and Syngman Rhee. Even in Europe, there was American support for the Greek junta.

Perhaps the most illuminating example here is the United States' stalwart support for another settler-apartheid regime, namely South Africa. The United States must share the blame for propping up and legitimizing the grossly authoritarian racism inflicted upon the South Africans. Of course, its foreign policy stance went lock, stock, and barrel with its own foundational history of genocide and slavery. Today, we're seeing a specifically American brand of fascism, which was previously only either exported internationally or inflicted upon racialized second-class or non-citizens domestically, now returning like the repressed, and finding its way into every facet of life, even that of its previously protected white citizenry.

Therefore, what my hero, the philosopher Simone Weil, said still holds true, whether the violent imperialism is emanating from across the Atlantic or the shores of the Mediterranean: "The great error of nearly all studies of war ... has been to consider war as an episode in foreign politics, when it is especially an act of interior politics, and the most atrocious act of all."[4] For Weil, war is a form of oppression, like prison or wage slavery, but at its most extreme and violent. So any oppression sent abroad always returns in domestic life.

Even if it has not been explicitly stated, the students spearheading today's nationwide protest movement grasp this principle. It may be on an entirely intuitive level, but it is understood. They, the students, which includes you all, have mobilized according to a sentiment opposing war and oppression. What you are all doing happens to be a demonstration of an equally valid principle from the Talmud that states whoever saves a single life is considered to have saved the entire world.[5]

Furthermore, whether or not you have recognized it, you have all entered into a transgenerational struggle on the side of justice. You have inserted yourself into history on the right side of it, on the side battling against oppression. For this reason alone, I want to express my total and complete solidarity with all of you and commend you for your victory today on campus!

The year 2023 was distinguished as one of the bloodiest years in recent memory for those living on the other side of the wall and on the bank of the river. This repressive violence was clearly a reaction to the new forms of unified struggle amongst the oppressed. This new unity started to emerge after the Great March in 2018 and even more so after the 2021 Unity uprising. I visited to learn first-hand about how this unity expressed itself in new forms of organization. Later, I would come to learn that the name for what I was trying to understand is a concept that is variously translated as the unity of "squares," "fields," "arenas," or "fronts."

Even from those who are sympathetic, you don't hear enough about these kinds of theoretical innovations. Of course, we are all against the geno-cide. But it would be a huge error to simply view the persecuted, the targeted, the massacred as victims alone.[6] In other words, there is a seventy-five-year history of active resistance and struggle that should not be overlooked. What's more, it is a tradition that has managed to change and grow with time.

Rather than passive victims, it is important to recognize that they are active agents with lessons for all of us. Not at all objects, but subjects. In fact, they more than likely form the most advanced human configuration on the face of the planet earth. This is not to espouse some kind of ethnic essentialism here. Truth be told, since ethnicity is so closely tied to statehood, it is the exact opposite. As the paradigmatic stateless people, they show the world how to oppose the domination of the state as such. We are being shown the avant-garde in the fight for freedom. The expelled and the excluded constitute the vanguard of all people.[7] It is repeatedly displayed in their unwavering, undaunting, and continual struggle for liberation. Furthermore, it is crucial to incorporate this magnificent example into what we do here and elsewhere.

This new unity that has been forged is, however, not an all-inclusive unity without any reservations. There are formations that collaborate with the occupying state that cannot participate in this newly forged unity. Due to its role in participating in the repression of the resistance, the comprador-bourgeoisie government in the territories is rejected as essentially the same as any other occupying force. Consequently, despite being composed of those who might nominally be designated as having a certain identity shared with the oppressed, it is no longer considered to truly be of the same people.

This is precisely how the martyred thinker Bassel al-Araj conceived of the complexities of identity. He asserted that anyone who sees the oppressed as a part of their struggle can assume the identity of the oppressed, despite the "secondary identities" one is born with.[8] Specifically, if a person wholly throws themself into fighting against apartheid and occupation, then that person can be wholly identified with the occupied in revolt as opposed to the repressive occupier. It requires a complete transformation that would consume every vestige of a person's previous identification with the settlers and colonizers. It demands that someone always be on the front line of battle for the oppressed and constantly on duty in the struggle. This is the duty that white humanitarian tourists in the Holy Land reneged on. Whereas, at least today, you all did not fail to take up this responsibility!

As Adi Callai has brilliantly explained, Frantz Fanon had already developed a similar formulation to this: he argued that anyone fighting for decolonization could themself become an Algerian.[9] Accordingly, in some instances, Fanon insisted that the fight to completely end racism entailed that the division between Black and white would itself be destroyed. Similarly, Ali Shariati also maintained that the fundamental division was not so much rooted in race, ethnicity, or religion, but in the division of all of humanity and its history into two camps: Cain and Abel, the oppressor and oppressed.[10] Likewise, Bassel al-Araj would go on to claim that he had abandoned all socially mandated dualities and distinctions. For al-Araj, these crude binaries were a naive oversimplification of the struggle. In short, what each of the three thinkers is trying to get across is that everything breaks down into two camps: the camp of liberation versus the camp of colonialism. We therefore find people of every skin color in both.

The powers that be have done their best to reinstall other, less important divisions. This is why capitalist imperialism has recently been so insistent in its appeal to narratives of white victimhood even though there have been so many defections from the colonizer's camp. There is a struggle over the identity of the colonizer and over whiteness itself. The foundation of the settler state sought to transfigure a historically minoritarian identity into that of a dominant Western nationality. What the youth is doing in the streets and on the campuses is rejecting this by redefining themselves on their own terms. In aligning themselves with the side of liberation, they are drawing on a much older lineage of this minoritarian identity that dates back to biblical times. It reaches back to ancient religious narratives that recount the struggle against pharaonic slavery. Like the old spiritual goes, "Got to get my people out of Pharaoh's hand / And lead them over to the Promised Land." As so many radical theologians have never tired of repeating, this goal can only be accomplished when the Holy Land has ceased to be restricted to one nation state, but instead spans the entirety of the planet earth!

Notes

2. How It Might Should Be Done

1. This talk was originally given on July 20, 2020. The reference is to the previous night's events: "After several weeks of calm with low-key protests, demonstrators returned to downtown Seattle on July 19. Police reported that peaceful demonstrators began to gather in the morning at Westlake Park but three hours later they were joined by a second group that was organized and more intent on property destruction. Several buildings were vandalized and police officers were injured, before the protesters dispersed after marching to Cal Anderson Park." Wikipedia, "George Floyd Protests in Seattle," https://en.wikipedia.org/wiki/George_Floyd_protests_in_Seattle.

2. Nikolai Chernyshevsky, *What Is to Be Done?*, trans. Michael R. Katz (Cornell University Press, 1989).

3. Vladimir Lenin, "What Is to Be Done?," in *Essential Works of Lenin: "What Is to Be Done?" and Other Writings*, ed. Henry M. Christman (Dover, 1987).

4. Tiqqun, *This Is Not a Program*, trans. Joshua David Jordan (Semiotext(e), 2011).

5. Maureen Groppe and Kristine Phillips, "From Coastal Cities to Rural Towns, Breadth of George Floyd Protests—Most Peaceful—Captured by Data," *USA Today*, June 10, 2020, https://www.usatoday.com/story/news/politics/2020/06/10/geoge-floyd-black-lives-matter-police-protests-widespread-peaceful/5325737002/.

6. William Barr describes the protests as "senseless acts of anarchy." "George Floyd Protests: Barr Says They Have Evidence

'Extremist Groups' Involved with Violent Activity," video clip, from US Department of Justice press conference, posted June 4, 2020, by Global News, YouTube, https://youtu.be/YHZUs2zr4Ng.

7. Wikipedia, "2020 Deployment of Federal Forces in the United States," https://en.wikipedia.org/wiki/2020_deployment_of_federal_forces_in_the_United_States.

8. Peggy McIntosh, "White Privilege: Unpacking the Invisible Knapsack," *Peace & Freedom*, July/August 1989, 10–12.

9. Chris Chen, Idris Robinson, Iyko Day, John Clegg, Sarika Chandra, and Shellyne Rodriguez, "Racial Capitalism & Disposable Populations in the Time of COVID," moderated by Chris Nealon, panel discussion, live streamed May 15, 2020, by Red May TV, YouTube, https:/youtu.be/MHMeYtYHiKM.

10. James Baldwin, *Going to Meet the Man* (Vintage Books, 1995).

11. Emily Badger, Claire Cain Miller, Adam Pearce, and Kevin Quealy, "Extensive Data Shows Punishing Reach of Racism for Black Boys," *New York Times*, March 19, 2018, https://www.nytimes.com/interactive/2018/03/19/upshot/race-class-white-and-black-men.html.

12. John Clegg, "How Slavery Shaped American Capitalism," *Jacobin*, August 28, 2019, https://jacobin.com/2019/08/how-slavery-shaped-american-capitalism.

13. Mårten Björk, "Phase Two—the Reproduction of This Life," *Tillfällighetsskrivande* (blog), June 23, 2020, archived September 19, 2020, at https://web.archive.org/web/20200919145917/https://www.tillfallighet.org/tillfallighetsskrivande/phase-two-the-reproduction-of-this-life.

14. The Invisible Committee, *To Our Friends*, trans. Robert Hurley (Semiotext(e), 2014).

15. *Preparedness 101: Zombie Pandemic* (Centers for Disease Control and Prevention, US Department of Health and Human Services, 2011), https://stacks.cdc.gov/view/cdc/6023.

16. Wikipedia, "2020 Twitter Account Hijacking," https://en.wikipedia.org/wiki/2020_Twitter_account_hijacking.

17. Kenneth Rexroth, *An Autobiographical Novel*, ed. Linda Hamalian (New Directions, 1991).

18. W. E. B. Du Bois, *Black Reconstruction in America* (Free Press, 1998).

19. Pier Paolo Pasolini, *In Danger: A Pasolini Anthology*, ed. Jack Hirschman (City Lights, 2010).

20. Walter Benjamin, "Theses on the Concept of History," in *Illuminations*, ed. Hannah Arendt, trans. Harry Zohn (Schocken Books, 1968).

3. Race Traitors, Identity Politics, and Revolutionary Horizons Since the George Floyd Uprising (HIMSBD 2.0)

1. James Boggs, *American Revolution: Pages from a Negro Worker's Notebook* (Monthly Review Press, 1963).

2. Guy Debord, *Comments on the Society of the Spectacle*, trans. Malcolm Imrie (Verso, 1998).

3. Alain Badiou, *Logics of Worlds: Being and Event II*, trans. Alberto Toscano (Continuum, 2009).

4. Guy Debord, *In Girum Imus Nocte et Consumimur Igni*, film soundtrack, trans. Ken Knabb, Bureau of Public Secrets, http://www.bopsecrets.org/SI/debord.films/ingirum.htm.

5. Cornel West, "Philosophy and the Afro-American Experience," in *A Companion to African-American Philosophy*, ed. Tommy L. Lott and John P. Pittman (Wiley, 2006).

6. This talk was given in a suburb of Detroit.

7. Idris Robinson, "The Destituent Urge Is Also a Destructive Urge: Agamben, Aristotle, and Benjamin on the Potentiality of Destitution," in this volume.

8. This is a reference to Agamben's and Badiou's objections concerning Jacques Rancière's notion of a "part of those who have no part."

See Giorgio Agamben, *The Time That Remains: A Commentary on the Letter to the Romans*, trans. Patricia Dailey (Stanford University Press, 2005), 58; and Alain Badiou, "Rancière and Apolitics," in *Metapolitics*, trans. Jason Barker (Verso, 2005), 114–23.

9. Kimberlé Crenshaw, "Mapping the Margins: Intersectionality, Identity Politics, and Violence Against Women of Color," *Stanford Law Review* 43, no. 6 (1991): 1241–99.

10. McIntosh, "White Privilege."

11. Cressida Heyes, "Identity Politics," in *Stanford Encyclopedia of Philosophy* (Stanford University, 1997–), published July 16, 2002; substantive revision November 1, 2024, https://plato.stanford.edu/entries/identity-politics/.

12. Stanley Cavell, "Excursus on Wittgenstein's Vision of Language," in *The New Wittgenstein*, ed. Alice Crary and Rupert Read (Routledge, 2000).

13. Gilles Deleuze and Félix Guattari, *A Thousand Plateaus*, trans. Brian Massumi (Bloomsbury, 2014); and Gilles Deleuze and Félix Guattari, *Anti-Oedipus: Capitalism and Schizophrenia*, trans. Robert Hurley (Penguin Books, 2009).

14. Toni Cade Bambara, ed., *The Black Woman: An Anthology* (Washington Square Press, 2005).

15. Robert Bernasconi, *Critical Philosophy of Race: Essays* (Oxford University Press, 2023).

16. David Marriott, *On Black Men* (Columbia University Press, 2000).

17. Baldwin, *Going to Meet the Man*.

18. Hortense J. Spillers, "Mama's Baby, Papa's Maybe: An American Grammar Book," in *Black, White, and in Color: Essays on American Literature and Culture* (University of Chicago Press, 2003).

19. Harriet Jacobs, *Incidents in the Life of a Slave Girl* (Harvard University Press, 1987).

20. Spillers, "Mama's Baby, Papa's Maybe," 222.

21. Jacobs, *Life of a Slave Girl*.

22. Simone Weil, "Reflections on War," *Journal of Continental Philosophy* 1, no. 2 (2021): 93–103.

23. Daniel McLoughlin, "Giorgio Agamben on Security, Government and the Crisis of Law," *Griffith Law Review* 21, no. 3 (2012): 680–707; and Ernst Jünger, *Storm of Steel*, trans. Michael Hofmann (Penguin Books, 2004).

24. Andrew Lakoff, "'The Supply Chain Must Continue': Becoming Essential in the Pandemic Emergency," *Items*, November 5, 2020, https://items.ssrc.org/covid-19-and-the-social-sciences/disaster-studies/the-supply-chain-must-continue-becoming-essential-in-the-pandemic-emergency.

25. Andrew Lakoff, *Unprepared: Global Health in the Time of Emergency* (University of California Press, 2017).

26. Michel Foucault, *Security, Territory, Population: Lectures at the Collège de France, 1977–1978*, ed. Michel Senellart, trans. Graham Burchell (Picador, 2007).

27. Silvia Federici, *Caliban and the Witch* (Autonomedia, 2004).

28. Carlo Ginzburg, *The Cheese and the Worms: The Cosmos of a Sixteenth-Century Miller*, trans. Anne Tedeschi (Johns Hopkins University Press, 2013).

29. Sonali Gupta and H. Bolin, "Virality: Against a Standard Unit of Life," *e-flux journal*, no. 115 (February 2021): https://www.e-flux.com/journal/115/373014/virality-against-a-standard-unit-of-life/.

30. The Invisible Committee, *To Our Friends*.

31. Louis Auguste Blanqui, *The Blanqui Reader: Political Writings, 1830–1880*, ed. Philippe Le Goff, Peter Hallward, and Mitchell Abidor (Verso, 2018).

32. Edward Luttwak, *Coup d'État: A Practical Handbook* (Harvard University Press, 2016).

33. Harry Haywood, *Black Bolshevik: Autobiography of an Afro-American Communist* (Liberator, 1978).

34. Nicole Loraux, *The Divided City: On Memory and Forgetting in Ancient Athens*, trans. Corinne Pache and Jeff Fort (Zone Books, 2002).

35. Shemon Salam and Arturo Castillon, "Prelude to a New Civil War," in *The Revolutionary Meaning of the George Floyd Uprising* (Daraja, 2021), 18–30.

36. David W. Blight, "15. Lincoln, Leadership, and Race: Emancipation as Policy," course lecture, for The Civil War and Reconstruction (HIST 119), posted November 21, 2008, by YaleCourses, YouTube, https://youtu.be/2YKZ1bI5C44.

37. W. E. B. Du Bois, "John Brown and Christmas," *The Horizon: A Journal of the Color Line* 5, no. 2 (December 1909): 1.

38. Giorgio Agamben, *The Time That Remains*; and Jacob Taubes, *The Political Theology of Paul*, trans. Dana Hollander (Stanford University Press, 2008).

39. Rodrigo Karmy Bolton, *Intifada: Una topología de la imaginación popular* (Metales Pesados, 2020).

40. Karmy Bolton, *Intifada*.

4. Letter to Michael Reinoehl

1. "Man Linked to Killing at a Portland Protest Says He Acted in Self-Defense," newscast, posted September 3, 2020, by VICE News, YouTube, https://youtu.be/fsDWXx5tYfk.

2. Walter Benjamin, *Toward the Critique of Violence: A Critical Edition*, ed. Peter Fenves and Julia Ng (Stanford University Press, 2021), 58–59.

3. This is a reference to Sun Tzu's notion of 死地 or *sǐ dì*, which can be rendered as "death-ground." See Sun Tzu, "The Nine Situations," in *The Art of War*, trans. Samuel B. Griffith (Oxford University Press, 1963).

4. *John Brown's Holy War*, directed by Robert Kenner, aired February 28, 2000, on PBS.

5. Ron Hahne and Ben Morea, *Black Mask & Up Against the Wall Motherfucker: The Incomplete Works of Ron Hahne, Ben Morea, and the Black Mask Group* (PM Press, 2011), 141.

5. The Poor Man's Luigi

1. J. David Goodman, "Order, Chaos and T-Shirts," *City Room* (blog), *New York Times*, May 3, 2010, https://archive.nytimes.com/cityroom.blogs.nytimes.com/2010/05/03/order-chaos-and-t-shirts/.

2. Bruce Reynolds, *The Autobiography of a Thief* (Bantam, 1995), 140.

3. See Sean Gardiner, "Cops on Steroids," *Village Voice*, December 11, 2007, https://www.villagevoice.com/cops-on-steroids/.

4. Marcus Tullius Cicero, *Laelius de Amicitia*, ed. C. F. W. Müller (Teubner, 1884), VI.22.

5. Hubert Selby Jr., *Requiem for a Dream* (Thunder's Mouth, 1978), 276.

6. Mos Def, "Mathematics," track 16 on *Black on Both Sides*, Rawkus, 1999.

7. Guy Debord, *Panegyric*, vol. 1, trans. James Brook, in *Panegyric: Volumes 1 & 2* (Verso, 2004), 37–38.

8. See David Kishik, *The Manhattan Project: A Theory of the City* (Stanford University Press, 2015).

9. See Paul Martinka, Georgett Roberts, and Gabrielle Fonrouge, "Brooklyn 'Zombieland' Bodega Shut Down by Sheriff," *New York Post*, January 22, 2020, https://nypost.com/2020/01/22/brooklyn-zombieland-bodega-shut-down-by-sheriff/.

10. Cannibal Ox, "Iron Galaxy," track 1 on *The Cold Vein*, Def Jux, 2001.

11. *Piñero*, directed by Leon Ichaso (Miramax, 2001).

12. Cannibal Ox, "Iron Galaxy."

6. Postscript: On Pain

1. Anne Case and Angus Deaton, *Deaths of Despair and the Future of Capitalism* (Princeton University Press, 2020), 84.

2. Case and Deaton, *Deaths of Despair*, 83.

3. Debord, *In Girum Imus Nocte*.

4. Debord, *In Girum Imus Nocte*.

5. Debord, *In Girum Imus Nocte*.

6. Pier Paolo Pasolini, *Saggi sulla politica e sulla società* (Mondadori, 1999), 589.

7. Debord, *In Girum Imus Nocte*.

8. Debord, *In Girum Imus Nocte*.

9. *Pain: Current Understanding of Assessment, Management, and Treatments* (National Pharmaceutical Council, 2021), 4.

10. *Pain*, 4.

7. The Revolt Eclipses Whatever the World Has to Offer

1. Dimitris Chatzivasileiadis, "Response to the Week of Revenge for Comrade Michael Forest Reinoehl, Who Was Murdered by Government Order," *Abolition Media* (blog), May 30, 2022, https://abolitionmedia.noblogs.org/839/.

2. Mario Tronti, "Towards a Critique of Political Democracy," trans. Alberto Toscano, *Cosmos and History: The Journal of Natural and Social Philosophy* 5, no. 1 (2009): 68–75.

3. Niccolò Machiavelli, *The Prince*, trans. George Bull (Penguin Classics, 2003).

4. Karmy Bolton, *Intifada*.

5. Gerardo Muñoz, "Going Nowhere: On Jason E. Smith's *Smart Machines and Service Work* (2020)," *Infrapolitical Reflections* (blog), January 14, 2021, https://infrapoliticalreflections.org/2021/01/14/going-nowhere-on-jason-e-smiths-smart-machines-and-service-work-2021-by-gerardo-munoz/.

6. Shemon, Arturo, and Atticus, "Fire on Main Street: Small Cities in the George Floyd Uprising," *It's Going Down*, January 4, 2021, https://itsgoingdown.org/fire-on-main-street-small-cities-in-the-george-floyd-uprising/.

7. Rodrigo Karmy Bolton, "The Anarchy of Beginnings: Notes on the Rhythmicity of Revolt," *Ill Will*, May 7, 2020, https://illwill.com/the-anarchy-of-beginnings.

9. Introduction to Mario Tronti's "On Destituent Power"

1. Idris Robinson, Richard Braude, Ricardo Andrés Guzmán, and Gerardo Muñoz, "There Is No Unhappy Revolution," moderated by Bella Bravo, panel discussion, live streamed May 26, 2021, by Red May TV, YouTube, https://youtu.be/BP1h4jOBPmw.

2. Mario Tronti, "Our Operaismo," *New Left Review* 73 (January/February 2012): https://newleftreview.org/issues/ii73/articles/mario-tronti-our-operaismo.pdf; and Mario Tronti, "I Am Defeated," interview by Antonio Gnoli, trans. Rees Nicolas, *Communists In Situ* (blog), March 3, 2015, https://cominsitu.wordpress.com/2015/03/08/mario-tronti-i-am-defeated/.

3. Amadeo Bordiga, "The Naples Meeting of the International Communist Party—September 1, 1951: Summary," in *Lessons of the Counterrevolutions*, Libcom.org, published December 6, 2013, https://libcom.org/article/lessons-counterrevolutions-amadeo-bordiga.

4. Sean Bonney, "Rimbaud and the Paris Commune," *The Commune* (blog), November 19, 2010, https://thecommune.wordpress.com/2010/11/19/rimbaud-and-the-paris-commune/.

5. Karl Marx, "Letter from Marx to Arnold Ruge: In Dresden," May 1843, Marxists Internet Archive, https://www.marxists.org/archive/marx/works/1843/letters/43_05-alt.htm.

6. Walter Benjamin, "Surrealism," in *Reflections: Essays, Aphorisms, Autobiographical Writings*, ed. Peter Demetz, trans. Edmund Jephcott (Schocken Books, 1978), 190.

7. For more on the decline of socialist reformism within the context of the past decades neoliberal offensive, see Gilles Dauvé and Karl

Nesic, *Whither the World*, Libcom.org, published February 16, 2007, https://libcom.org/article/whither-world-gilles-dauve-karl-nesic.

8. Michael Löwy, *Fire Alarm: Reading Walter Benjamin's "On the Concept of History,"* trans. Chris Turner, (Verso, 2005), 37.

9. Löwy, *Fire Alarm*, 30.

10. This is but one of many disagreements between the two dating back to the dissolution of the *Classe operaia* journal in 1967, which signaled an end to their collective partnership in theoretical pursuits. See Steve Wright, *Storming Heaven: Class Composition and Struggle in Italian Autonomist Marxism* (Pluto, 2002), 221–25.

11. Antonio Negri, "Interpretation of the Class Situation Today: Methodological Aspects," in *Open Marxism*, vol. 2, *Theory and Practice*, ed. Werner Bonefeld, Richard Gunn, and Kosmas Psychopedis (Pluto, 1992), theses 4–5 (p. 75–79), 8 (p. 82–85), 10 (p. 86–87), 12 (p. 90–91), 17 (p. 98–100).

12. On this point, see Aufheben, "From *Operaismo* to 'Autonomist Marxism': A Response," Libcom.org, published July 24, 2005, https://libcom.org/article/operaismo-autonomist-marxism.

13. Mario Tronti, "We Have Populism Because There Is No People," trans. David Broder, *Verso* (blog), March 27, 2013, https://www.versobooks.com/blogs/news/1261-mario-tronti-we-have-populism-because-there-is-no-people.

14. Tronti, "Critique of Political Democracy."

10. The Destituent Urge Is Also a Destructive Urge: Agamben, Aristotle, and Benjamin on the Potentiality of Destitution

1. Early drafts of this article were presented at the University of New Mexico, Indiana University, Red May Seattle, and an outdoor public event in Olympia, Washington, during the George Floyd uprising.

2. Roughly the same demand was later echoed during the Arab Spring with the chant "Ash-sha'b yurīd isqāt an-nizām!" (The people want to bring down the regime!).

3. Colectivo Situaciones, *19 & 20: Notes for a New Social Protagonism*, trans. Nate Holdren and Sebastián Touza (Minor Compositions, 2011), 52.

4. Antonio Negri, *Insurgencies: Constituent Power and the Modern State*, trans. Maurizia Boscagli (University of Minnesota Press, 1999), 1–34.

5. Emmanuel Joseph Sieyès, "What Is the Third Estate?," trans. Michael Sonenscher, in *Political Writings: Including the Debate Between Sieyès and Tom Paine in 1791*, ed. Michael Sonenscher (Hackett, 2003), 92–162; and Martin Loughlin, "On Constituent Power," in *Constitutionalism Beyond Liberalism*, ed. Michael W. Dowdle and Michael A. Wilkinson (Cambridge University Press, 2017), 151–56.

6. Mario Tronti, "Sul potere destituente: Discussione con Mario Tronti," in *Pouvoir destituente: Le rivolte metropolitane*, ed. Pierandrea Amato, Tristana Dini, Paolo Primi, Luca Salza, and Adriano Vinale (Mimesis, 2008), 23–32.

7. See the timeline authored by contributors from the *Hostis* journal: "Destituent Power: An Incomplete Timeline," *Destituencies*, no. 0 (November 2020): archived November 1, 2020, at https://web.archive.org/web/20201101134946/https://destituencies.com/2020/destituent-power-an-incomplete-timeline/.

8. Giorgio Agamben, "What Is a Destituent Power?," trans. Stephanie Wakefield, *Environment and Planning D: Society and Space* 32, no. 1 (February 2014): 70.

9. Agamben, "What Is a Destituent Power?," 71.

10. Giorgio Agamben, *The Use of Bodies: Homo Sacer IV, 2*, trans. Adam Kotsko (Stanford University Press, 2016), 268.

11. Giorgio Agamben, *Homo Sacer: Sovereign Power and Bare Life*, trans. Daniel Heller-Roazen (Stanford University Press, 1998), 44–48; and Giorgio Agamben, "The Power of Thought," trans. Kalpana Seshadri, *Critical Inquiry* 40, no. 2 (Winter 2014): 480–91.

12. Aristotle, *Metaphysics*, ed. W. D. Ross (Clarendon, 1924), 1019a34, 1046a5. Unless otherwise indicated, all translations from Greek are my own.

13. Agamben, "The Power of Thought," 487.

14. Agamben, "The Power of Thought," 483.

15. Aristotle, *De Anima*, ed. W. D. Ross (Clarendon, 1956), 417a21–b1, 429b5–9; and see also Aristotle, *Physics*, ed. W. D. Ross (Oxford University Press, 1936), 255a33–34 .

16. Martin Heidegger, Aristotle's *"Metaphysics* Θ *1–3": On the Essence and Actuality of Force*, trans. Walter Brogan and Peter Warnek (Indiana University Press, 1995).

17. Aristotle, *Metaphysics*, 1046b29.

18. Aristotle, *Metaphysics*, 1046b33.

19. Aristotle, *Metaphysics*, 1047a7–17.

20. Aristotle, *Metaphysics*, 1046a18.

21. Agamben, *Homo Sacer*, 45.

22. Aristotle, *Metaphysics*, 1046a32.

23. Aristotle, *Metaphysics*, 1050a10. For the sake of consistency, I have here followed the translation in Agamben, *Homo Sacer*, 45.

24. Kevin Attell, "Potentiality, Actuality, Constituent Power," *Diacritics* 39, no. 3 (Fall 2009): 40.

25. Aristotle, *Metaphysics*, 1047a24–26.

26. Aristotle, *Categoriae et Liber de Interpretatione*, ed. L. Minio-Paluello (Oxford University Press, 1936), 21b.

27. Agamben, *Homo Sacer*, 47.

28. Agamben, *The Time That Remains*, 88–112.

29. Agamben, *The Time That Remains*, 95–99.

30. Agamben, *The Time That Remains*, 98.

31. Agamben, *The Time That Remains*, 95.

32. Agamben, *The Time That Remains*, 96.

33. Agamben, *The Time That Remains*, 97.

34. Agamben, *The Time That Remains*, 97.

35. Agamben, *The Time That Remains*, 98.

36. Agamben does, in fact, later acknowledge this sense of *ērgon* as a "product" or "result." Agamben, *The Use of Bodies*, 13–15.

37. Aristotle, *Metaphysics*, 1048a37. See Chung-Hwan Chen, "Different Meanings of the Term Energeia in the *Philosophy of Aristotle*," *Philosophy and Phenomenological Research* 17, no. 1 (September 1956): 56–65.

38. Aristotle, *Metaphysics*, 1048b7.

39. Aristotle, *Metaphysics*, 1048a35.

40. Aristotle, *Metaphysics*, 1048b4–31, 1050a7–27.

41. Aristotle, *Protrepticus, or Exhortation to Philosophy*, ed. and trans. D. S. Hutchinson and Monte Ransome Johnson (pub. by editors, 2017), B68–70, http://www.protrepticus.info/protr2017x20.pdf; Aristotle, *Eudemian Ethics*, ed. F. Susemihl (Teubner, 1884), 1219a; and Aristotle, *Nicomachean Ethics*, ed. J. Bywater (Clarendon, 1894), 1094–1095, 1098b31.

42. Aristotle, *Metaphysics*, 1050a24–37.

43. See Stephen John Zylstra, "Immanent Causation in Spinoza and Scholasticism" (PhD diss., University of Toronto, 2018).

44. *Poioumēno* is the present, middle-passive, dative participle of *poiēo*.

45. Aristotle, *Metaphysics*, 1050b13.

46. Aristotle, *Metaphysics*, 1018a20; and see also Aristotle, *Physics*, 201a10–15.

47. See Guy Debord, *The Society of the Spectacle*, trans. Donald Nicholson-Smith (Zone Books, 1994), theses 5 (p. 12–13), 8 (p.

14), 19–20 (p. 17–18), 32 (p. 23), 212–21 (p. 150–54). See also the endorsements of Debord's conception on the spectacular reification in Giorgio Agamben, *Means Without End: Notes on Politics*, trans. Vincenzo Binetti and Ceasare Casarino (University of Minnesota Press, 2000), 73–90; and the prologue to Giorgio Agamben, *The Use of Bodies*, xv–xxi.

48. In my view, these tensions are also indicated by a recent and rather dramatic shift in Agamben's interpretation of Aristotelian potentiality. For instance, in *Homo Sacer*, Agamben states, "It is never clear, to a reader freed from the prejudices of tradition, whether Book Theta of the *Metaphysics* in fact gives primacy to actuality or to potentiality" (47). However, the ninth chapter of Book Theta is devoted to showing how actuality is better (*beltīon*) and valued higher (*timiotēra*) than potentiality. Hence, there is an abrupt change in *The Use of Bodies*, in which Agamben comes to admit Aristotle's preference for actuality: "[Aristotle] thinks potential as existing in itself … and act as ontologically superior and prior" (276).

49. Agamben, *The Use of Bodies*, 13.

50. Dale B. Martin, *New Testament History and Literature* (Yale University Press, 2012), 231–46.

51. Benjamin, *Critique of Violence*, 48.

52. Benjamin, *Critique of Violence*, 48.

53. Benjamin, *Critique of Violence*, 55–56.

54. Benjamin, *Critique of Violence*, 55.

55. Sami Khatib, "Towards a Politics of 'Pure Means': Walter Benjamin and the Question of Violence," in *Conflicto armado, justicia y memoria*, ed. Enán Arrieta Burgos, vol. 1, *Teoría crítica de la violencia y prácticas de memoria y resistencia* (Editorial Universidad Pontificia Bolivariana, 2016), 45.

56. Benjamin, *Critique of Violence*, 57.

57. Benjamin, *Critique of Violence*, 60.

58. Benjamin, *Critique of Violence*, 54.

59. Benjamin, *Critique of Violence*, 44, 53–54, 58–59.

60. Giorgio Agamben, *State of Exception*, trans. Kevin Attell (University of Chicago Press, 2005), 54, 59–60, 63.

61. Immanuel Kant, *Groundwork of the Metaphysics of Morals*, ed. and trans. Mary Gregor (Cambridge University Press, 1998), 4:428 (p. 36).

62. Benjamin, *Critique of Violence*, 43.

63. Benjamin, *Critique of Violence*, 52.

64. Agamben, *State of Exception*, 61.

65. Agamben, *State of Exception*, 61.

66. Agamben, *State of Exception*, 62.

67. Agamben, *State of Exception*, 64.

68. Benjamin, *Critique of Violence*, 52.

69. Benjamin, *Critique of Violence*, 52.

70. Benjamin, *Critique of Violence*, 52–53. The only counterevidence is Benjamin's classification of the proletarian strike as nonviolent (*gewaltos*), but he is referring not to the action implicit within its pure means but to the fact that its rejection of reform entails that it refuses to reinstate the violence of capitalist labor and production.

71. Benjamin, *Critique of Violence*, 55.

72. Benjamin, *Critique of Violence*, 44–45, 55–56.

73. Benjamin, *Critique of Violence*, 56.

74. Benjamin, *Critique of Violence*, 57.

75. Peter Fenves, introduction to Benjamin, *Critique of Violence*, 33.

76. Walter Benjamin, "The Destructive Character," trans. Rodney Livingstone, in *Selected Writings*, vol. 2, pt. 2, *1931–1934*, ed. Michael W. Jennings, Howard Eiland, and Gary Smith (Belknap Press of Harvard University Press, 1999), 542.

77. Benjamin, *Critique of Violence*, 55.

78. Benjamin, *Critique of Violence*, 54–55.

79. Benjamin, *Critique of Violence*, 54, 55.

80. Eli Friedlander, "Assuming Violence: A Commentary on Walter Benjamin's 'Critique of Violence,'" *Boundary 2* 42, no. 4 (2015): 165.

81. Benjamin, *Critique of Violence*, 55.

82. Benjamin, *Critique of Violence*, 57.

83. Benjamin, *Critique of Violence*, 57.

84. Friedlander, "Assuming Violence," 166.

85. Benjamin, *Critique of Violence*, 55.

86. Gil Anidjar, "Blutgewalt," *Oxford Literary Review* 31, no. 2 (2009): 165.

87. Benjamin, *Critique of Violence*, 57.

88. Benjamin, *Critique of Violence*, 57.

89. Benjamin, *Critique of Violence*, 57.

90. Benjamin, *Critique of Violence*, 83–84.

91. Benjamin, *Critique of Violence*, 54, 56.

92. It is useful, in this case, to compare Agamben's celebrated interpretation of the Tiananmen affair as consisting of "singularities [that] peacefully demonstrate their being in common" with Andrew Walder and Gong Xiaoxia's narrative, compiled from firsthand accounts, of conflictual proletarian self-activity, as well as internal class divisions amongst the protesters. Giorgio Agamben, *The Coming Community*, trans. Michael Hardt (University of

Minnesota Press, 1993), 86; and Andrew G. Walder and Gong Xiaoxia, "Workers in the Tiananmen Protests: The Politics of the Beijing Workers' Autonomous Federation," *Australian Journal of Chinese Affairs*, no. 29 (January 1993): 1–29.

93. Paul Mason, *Why It's Still Kicking Off Everywhere: The New Global Revolution* (Verso, 2013), 5–24.

94. Debord, *In Girum*.

95. Agamben, *The Coming Community*, 82–86; and Idris Robinson, "How It Might Should Be Done," in this volume.

11. Figs on God's Mountain

1. Aimé Césaire, *Discourse on Colonialism*, trans. Joan Pinkham (Monthly Review Press, 2001), 74–75.

2. See Agamben, *Means Without End*, 18–19.

3. Frantz Fanon, *The Wretched of the Earth*, trans. Constance Farrington (Grove, 1963), 245–46 (translation slightly modified).

4. Césaire, *Discourse on Colonialism*, 73.

5. Fanon, *Wretched of the Earth*, 246 (translation slightly modified).

12. At the Encampments

1. Ryszard Kapuściński, *The Soccer War*, trans. William Brand (Vintage International, 1992), 199.

2. Assata Shakur, *Assata: An Autobiography* (Lawrence Hill, 1987), 266–74.

3. Shakur, *Assata*, 268–72.

4. Simone Weil, "Reflections on War," Libcom.org, published February 18, 2023, https://libcom.org/article/reflections-war-simone-weil.

5. Mishnah Sanhedrin 4:5, Talmud Bavli.

6. See Mohammed El-Kurd, *Perfect Victims: And the Politics of Appeal* (Haymarket Books, 2025).

7. See Agamben, *Means Without End*, 24.

8. "Basil Al-Araj, Palestinian Martyr: 'Today's Wars Are Struggles Between Societies,'" *Workers World*, November 3, 2023, https://www.workers.org/2023/11/74595/.

9. Adi Callai, "Frantz Fanon vs Identity Politics," video essay, posted May 5, 2022, by Rev & Reve, YouTube, https://youtu.be/jl08808aC-0.

10. Ali Shariati, "The Philosophy of History: Cain and Abel," ICIT Digital Library, https://www.icit-digital.org/articles/the-philosophy-of-history-cain-and-abel.

ABOUT THE AUTHOR

Idris Robinson is a philosopher and writer from the New York hinterlands. For over a decade, he has written extensively on crisis, revolt, and political violence. He is currently an assistant professor of philosophy at Texas State University.